BIOMES ATLASES

TEMPERATE GRASSLANDS

Ben Hoare

 www.heinemannraintree.com
Visit our website to find out more information about Heinemann-Raintree books.

To order:
☎ Phone 888-454-2279
🖳 Visit www.heinemannraintree.com to browse our catalog and order online.

Published in 2011 by Heinemann-Raintree books, an imprint of Capstone Global Library, LLC, Chicago, Illinois

© 2011 The Brown Reference Group Ltd.

For The Brown Reference Group Ltd:
Editorial Director: Lindsey Lowe
Managing Editor: Tim Harris
Editor: Jolyon Goddard
Original consultant: Dr. Mark Hostetler,
Department of Wildlife Ecology and Conservation, University of Florida
Designers: Reg Cox, Joan Curtis
Picture researcher: Clare Newman
Production Director: Alastair Gourlay

Printed in the USA

ISBN: 978-1-432-94181-9; 978-1-432-94184-0 (set)
14 13 12 11 10
10 9 8 7 6 5 4 3 2 1

Library of Congress Cataloging-in-Publication Data

Hoare, Ben.
  Temperate grasslands / Ben Hoare.
    p. cm.—(Biomes atlases)
  Includes bibliographical references and index.
  ISBN 978-1-4329-4181-9 (hc)
  1. Grassland ecology—Juvenile literature. 2. Grassland ecology—Maps for children. I. Title.
  QH541.5.P7H6 2011
  577.4—dc22   2010013034

About this Book

This book's introductory pages describe the biomes of the world biomes and then the temperate grassland biome. The five main chapters look at aspects of temperate grassland: climate, plants, animals, people, and the future. Between the chapters are detailed maps that focus on key grassland areas. The map pages are shown in the contents in italics, *like this*. Exclamation-point icons on the map pages draw attention to regions where the biome or its wildlife is under threat. Throughout the book you'll also find boxed stories or fact files about temperate grassland. The icons here show what the boxes are about. Words in **bold** throughout the book are explained in the glossary at the end of the book. After the glossary is a list of books and websites for further research and an index, allowing you to locate subjects anywhere in the book.

 Climate

 People

 Plants

 Future

 Animals

 Facts

 Extinction

 Under Threat

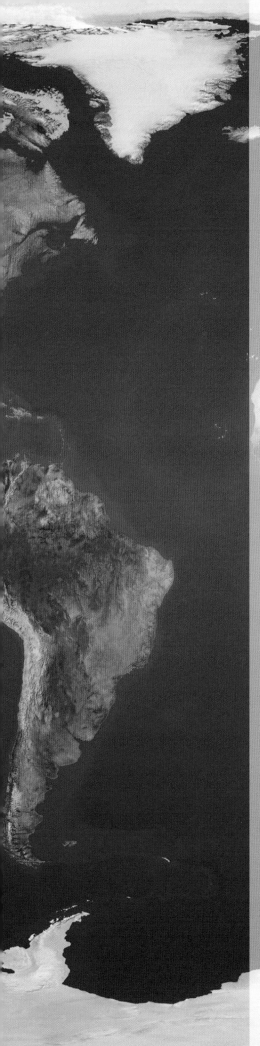

Contents

BIOMES OF THE WORLD

Biologists divide the living world into major zones named biomes. Each biome has its own distinctive climate, plants, and animals.

If you were to walk all the way from the north of Canada to the Amazon **rain forest**, you'd notice the wilderness changing dramatically along the way (see route marked on map to right).

Northern Canada is a freezing and barren place without trees, where only tiny brownish-green plants can survive in the icy ground. But trudge south for long enough and you enter a magical world of conifer forests, where moose, caribou, and wolves live. After several weeks, the conifers disappear, and you reach the grass-covered **prairies** of the central United States. The farther south you go, the drier the land gets and the hotter the sunshine feels, until you find yourself hiking through a cactus-filled **desert**. But once you reach southern Mexico, the cacti start to disappear, and strange **tropical** trees begin to take their place. Here, the muggy air is filled with the calls of exotic birds and the drone of tropical insects. Finally, in Colombia you cross the Andes mountain range—whose chilly peaks remind you a little of your starting point—and descend into the dense, swampy jungles of the Amazon rain forest.

Desert is the driest biome. There are hot deserts and cold ones.

Taiga is made up of conifer trees that can survive freezing winters.

Scientists have a special name for the different regions—such as desert, tropical rain forest, and prairie—that you'd pass through on such a journey. They call them **biomes**. Everywhere on Earth can be classified as being in one biome or another, and the same biome often appears in lots of different

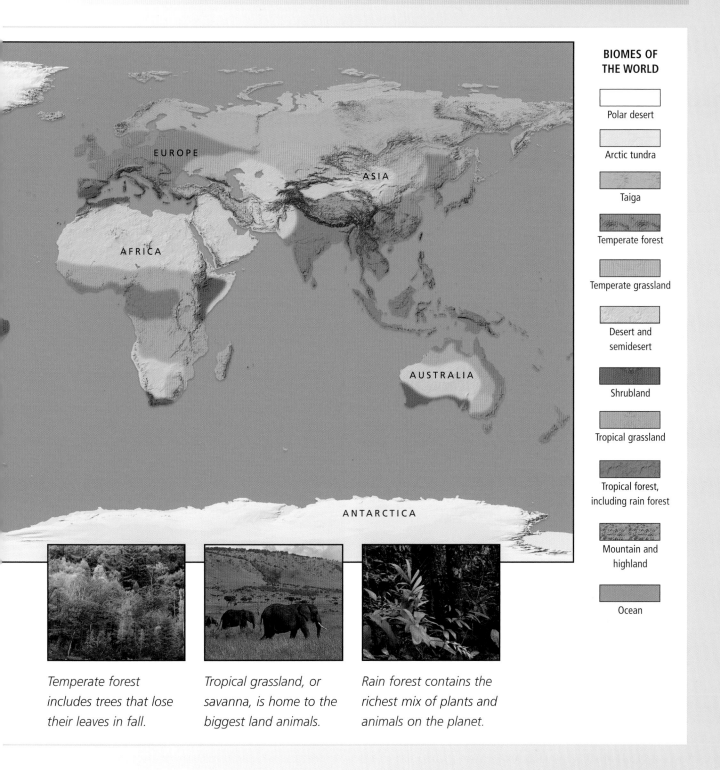

**BIOMES OF
THE WORLD**

Polar desert

Arctic tundra

Taiga

Temperate forest

Temperate grassland

Desert and
semidesert

Shrubland

Tropical grassland

Tropical forest,
including rain forest

Mountain and
highland

Ocean

EUROPE

ASIA

AFRICA

AUSTRALIA

ANTARCTICA

*Temperate forest
includes trees that lose
their leaves in fall.*

*Tropical grassland, or
savanna, is home to the
biggest land animals.*

*Rain forest contains the
richest mix of plants and
animals on the planet.*

places. For instance, there are areas of rain forest as far apart as Brazil, Africa, and Southeast Asia. Although the plants and animals inhabiting these forests are different, they live in similar ways. Likewise, the prairies of North America are part of the grassland biome, which also occurs in China, Australia, and Argentina. Wherever there are grasslands, there are grazing animals that feed on the grass, as well as large carnivores that hunt and kill the grazers.

The map on this page shows how the world's major biomes fit together to make up the biosphere—the zone of life on Earth.

TEMPERATE GRASSLANDS OF THE WORLD

Picture yourself standing alone in the middle of a massive field. Grass surrounds you on all sides. Now imagine the field has no fences or hedges and it goes on and on as far as the eye can see. That is grassland.

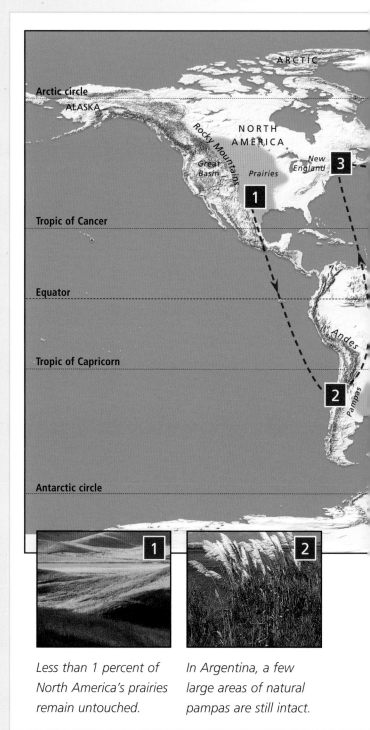

Less than 1 percent of North America's prairies remain untouched.

In Argentina, a few large areas of natural pampas are still intact.

In natural, unaltered **temperate grasslands**, grass stretches to the horizon in every direction, a sea of green that melts into the blue sky. In the shimmering heat haze it is difficult to tell where the grass ends and the sky begins. The landscape seems empty, and the only sounds are the hum of countless insects and the swishing of grass as it bends this way and that in the constant wind.

This is what grasslands are like in summer. The grasslands of the American West, called prairies, are big, flat, and open. At first, they can appear empty and lifeless, like a green desert. But this is an illusion—there is much more to prairies than meets the eye. Prairie is just one type of grassland. In South America

there are huge expanses of lush pasture called the **pampas**. **Veld** is the name for the grasslands that cover southern Africa, while the grassy plains of southeastern Australia are known as **rangeland**. Stretching across central Asia are the **steppes**, grasslands so vast they are clearly visible from space.

6

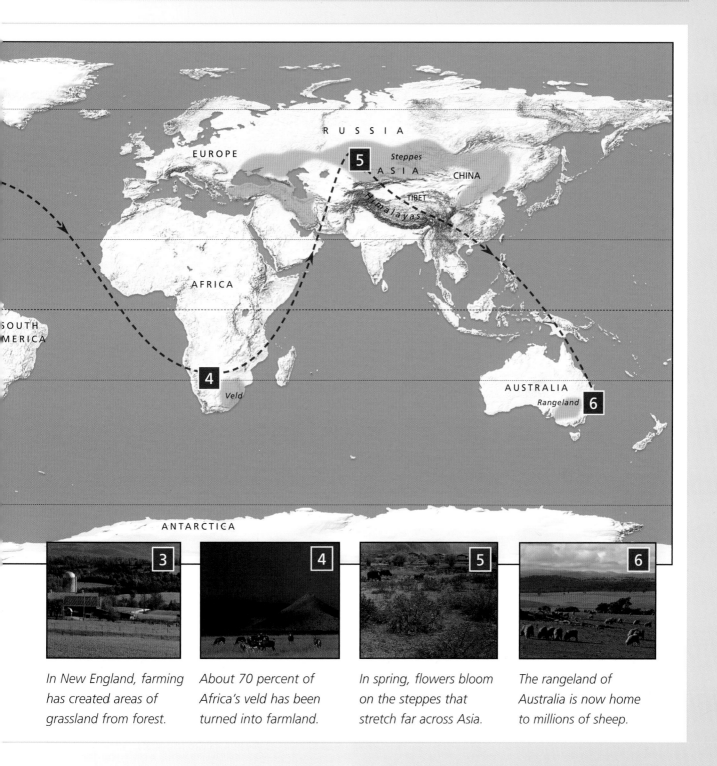

In New England, farming has created areas of grassland from forest.

About 70 percent of Africa's veld has been turned into farmland.

In spring, flowers bloom on the steppes that stretch far across Asia.

The rangeland of Australia is now home to millions of sheep.

All these grasslands belong to the temperate grassland biome. The word **temperate** describes their weather, which features warm summers and chilly winters. In summer it can get very hot, and in winter it may be freezing for days on end. However, temperate parts of the world are on average seldom as hot as the tropics or as cold as polar regions, but somewhere in between.

Temperate grasslands are one of the world's most important biomes. But, as this book explains, plants, animals, and people have to be tough to survive there. Life in temperate grasslands can be very hard indeed.

7

THE PRAIRIES

The prairies are at the crossroads of North America. They stretch from the Rocky Mountains east across the heart of the continent. These windswept lands now form one of the world's biggest farming regions.

Prairie Facts

▲ The prairie region covers an area of 2,900,000 square kilometers (1,125,000 square miles).

▲ Many scientists are worried that the prairies will become drier and turn into desert if global warming is not halted or reversed.

1. The Prairie Provinces
Fertile plains in the south of Alberta, Saskatchewan, and Manitoba mark the northern limit of the prairies. The northern short-grass prairie is the largest remaining natural grassland in North America.

2. Chimney Rock
Chimney Rock rises 150 meters (500 feet) above the grassy plain just to the south of the North Platte River in western Nebraska. This natural tower is all that's left of an ancient rocky plateau.

3. Potholes
Potholes are small ponds sunk into the northern prairies. They are scattered across a wide area, from eastern Montana to western Minnesota. They appear every spring as the snows melt, and provide a summer home for 100 species of birds. Frogs in the ponds are threatened by a highly contagious fungal disease.

4. The Badlands
Settlers found this wilderness of cliffs, crags, and gullies so hard to cross they named it the Badlands. It features strange rock formations created by years of wind and rain.

5. Hills of Sand
A dry zone of barely covered sandy hills and ridges lies in the middle of Nebraska.

6. Big Basin
This is an enormous hole in the plains of west Kansas, created when a series of huge caverns collapsed. It is 1.6 kilometers (1 mile) wide and 33 meters (100 feet) deep. Famed for its flowers, this mixed grass prairie is home to many birds, including western meadowlarks.

7. Salt Plains
In northern Oklahoma there are plains of white salt that stretch for 116 square kilometers (45 square miles). They are the remains of an ancient salt lake.

8. Wichita Mountains
The Wichita Mountains of western Oklahoma are 300 million years old—much older than the seas of grass that encircle them. This range includes a refuge for bison, elk, and deer. Wolves and bears were once native to the mountains but are now extinct here. Coyotes, pumas, and bobcats still remain but are threatened by human activities.

9. Flint Hills
The Flint Hills of eastern Kansas have steep grassy slopes and limestone crags. Along with the nearby Osage Hills, this is the last area of North America's unique tallgrass prairie. These hills were once home to vast herds of bison and elk. Prairie chickens live there, too.

10. Ozark Plateau
On the upland plains that cover much of central Missouri, ponderosa pines and spruce stands mix with the grass and small shrubs.

Prairie Chickens

Each spring, male prairie chickens get together in large groups, or leks. They rapidly stomp the ground and strut about making loud moans, clucks, and hoots. The aim of all this fuss is to attract female prairie chickens from the surrounding area. The females come to watch and mate with the best dancers. Prairie chickens are keystone species—they have an effect on many other species on the prairie, and their presence indicates that a prairie is in a healthy state. There are three species of prairie chickens, all which are at risk of extinction.

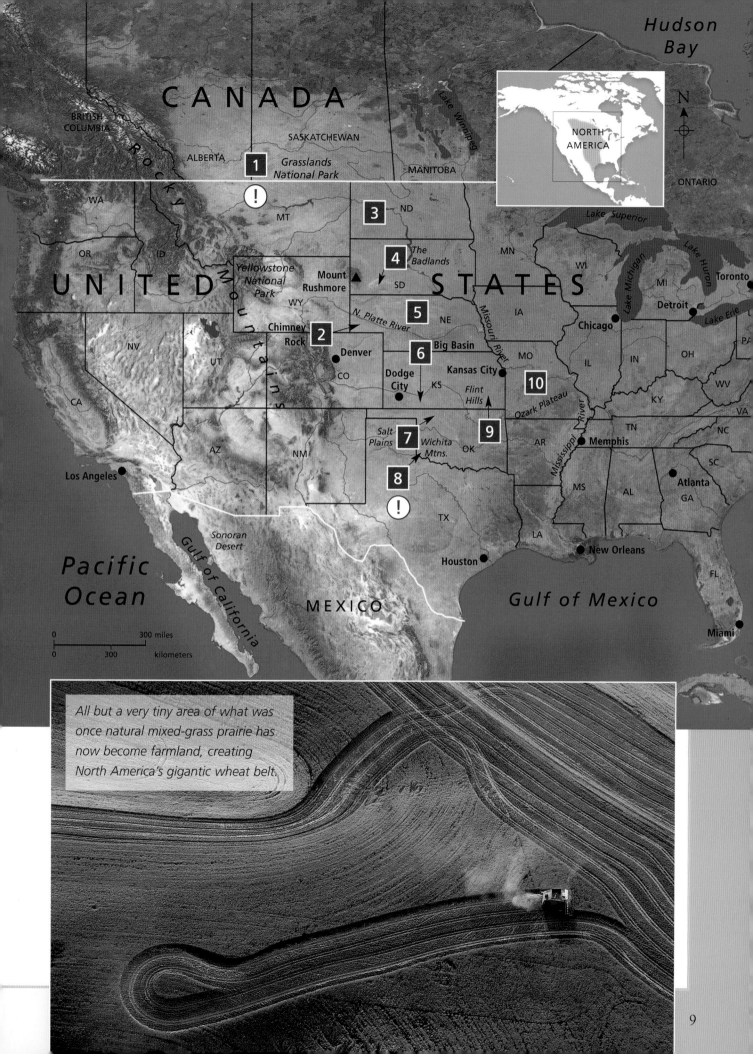

Hudson Bay

CANADA

BRITISH COLUMBIA

SASKATCHEWAN

ALBERTA

1 Grasslands National Park

MANITOBA

Lake Winnipeg

ONTARIO

NORTH AMERICA

N

WA

MT

3 ND

OR

ID

4 The Badlands

MN

Lake Superior

Lake Huron

UNITED

Yellowstone National Park

Mount Rushmore

SD

STATES

WI

MI

Lake Michigan

Toronto

Detroit

Lake Erie

WY

N. Platte River

NE

IA

Chicago

IL

IN

OH

PA

2 Chimney Rock

5

Missouri River

MO

6 Big Basin

Kansas City

10

WV

NV

UT

Denver

CO

Dodge City

KS

Flint Hills

Ozark Plateau

KY

VA

Mississippi River

TN

NC

9

AR

Memphis

SC

CA

AZ

NM

Salt Plains

7 Wichita Mtns.

OK

MS

AL

Atlanta

GA

8

TX

Los Angeles

Sonoran Desert

LA

Houston

New Orleans

FL

Pacific Ocean

Gulf of California

MEXICO

Gulf of Mexico

Miami

0   300 miles
0   300   kilometers

All but a very tiny area of what was once natural mixed-grass prairie has now become farmland, creating North America's gigantic wheat belt.

GRASSLAND CLIMATE

Temperate grasslands grow where there is not enough rain for forests but too much for a desert. With changeable weather and little shelter from the elements, they can be challenging places to live.

On a bright summer's day, anyone would think a temperate grassland is an easy place for plants and animals to live. It's likely to be pleasantly warm—not too hot, but just right. Often there is hardly a cloud in the sky and you can see for miles.

But this is not the whole story. Wide open spaces like grasslands are in fact harsh environments with a punishing **climate**. Climate means all the different types of weather that an area gets each year. In temperate grasslands the climate is dominated by nonstop change.

Fierce storms can break out at any time in grasslands, and when the weather changes for the worse, there's very little shelter to be found. Howling winds tear across the land, whipping up powerful dust storms in summer and raging **blizzards** in winter. Without a

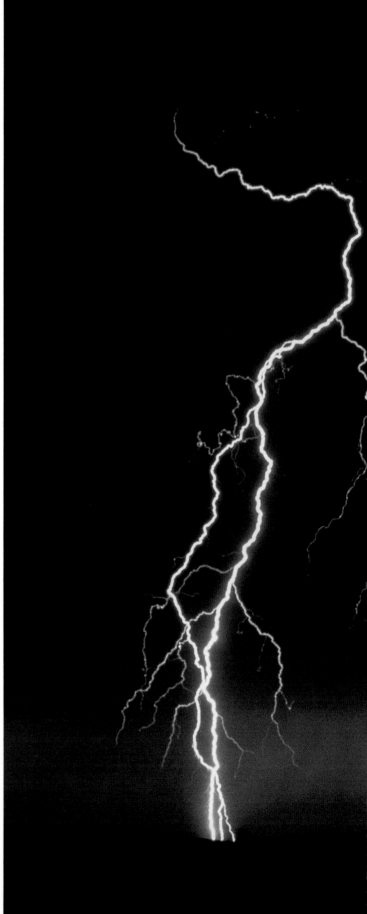

The cloudless skies of the grassland summer may be suddenly disturbed by violent storm fronts that sweep past, unleashing thunder and lightning.

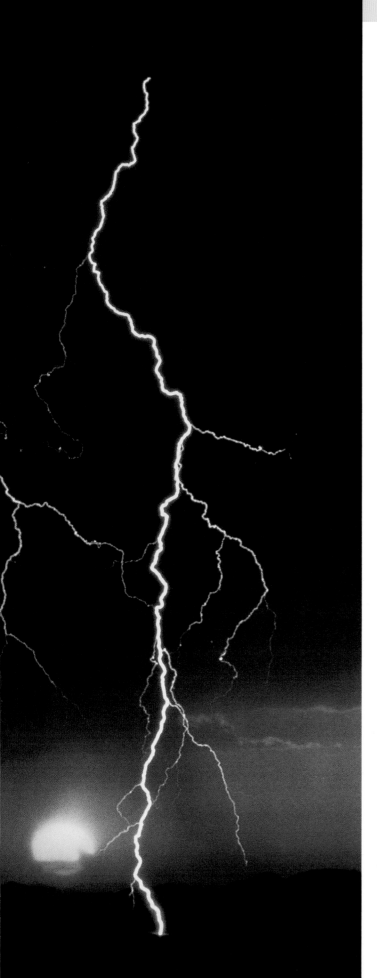

doubt, grasslands can be very unfriendly places indeed.

Great seas of grasses spread across the plains and rolling hills of every continent except Antarctica, where it is far too cold. This is a clue to where you find temperate grasslands—climate controls their location, as it does for most biomes. You normally find temperate grasslands in the center of continents far from the sea. They are temperate because they occur in the world's moderate, temperate zone—between the heat of the tropics and the cold of the poles.

Rain Control

More than anything else, it is rain that shapes the temperate grassland biome. The amount of rain that falls in a particular spot each year—the rainfall—decides which plants grow there. All plants need water to grow, and the wettest parts of the world have the greatest variety of plant life.

Lots of rain, or a high rainfall, allows trees and dense vegetation to thrive. Forests cover areas of high rainfall. If there is little rain, or a low rainfall, it is harder for plants to grow and trees cannot survive. Deserts occur in areas with the lowest rainfall. In places with more rain than deserts but less than forests, grasslands naturally take hold.

 Ice Bullets

Ferocious hailstorms batter the American prairies, spraying the ground like gunfire. Hail is frozen rain that forms inside supercooled clouds, but unlike snow it falls during the warmer months of the year. The heaviest hailstone ever reported in the United States crashed into Coffeyville, Kansas, on September 3, 1970. The giant lump of ice weighed 757 grams (1.7 pounds) and measured 19 centimeters (7.5 inches) across.

Changing Seasons

It is not only the amount of rain that determines where grasslands exist—the timing of the rain also matters. In prairies and other temperate grasslands, some times of the year are wetter than others. The rainiest seasons are late spring and early summer. Torrential downpours lash the ground, creating temporary pools and turning gentle streams into foaming white water. As much as 250 millimeters (10 inches) of water may cascade down in the space of a few hours. However, the rains don't last long, and soon the water soaks into the soil or drains away.

In late summer, the opposite happens. It drizzles but might not rain properly for several weeks or more. During the summer drought, the Sun's rays bake the earth and many streams dry up. There are occasional violent thunderstorms, but these are short lived. The remote steppes of inland Asia suffer the most devastating droughts of all. Sometimes, hardly a drop of rain falls for long periods, transforming the green and pleasant land into a dry and dusty world.

Lands of Extremes

Wild swings in temperature are another crucial feature of temperate grasslands. On the steppes of Mongolia, for example, daytime temperatures soar to more than 38°C (100°F) in midsummer and dive to −18°C (0°F) or lower in winter.

Just like the spring rainstorms, the cold spells often arrive without warning. Grassy plains may vanish under a thick blanket of snow for kilometers around. On other occasions the snows melt almost as quickly as they came. During summer, frequent heatwaves scorch the land. Such dramatic changes in the weather test the endurance of plants, animals, and people.

Blowing in the Wind

Strong winds make life difficult on grasslands, blasting everything in sight. The wind blows harder and longer in the prairies than anywhere else in the United States. It is almost always windy in temperate grasslands because the country is so flat and exposed. There are not enough trees to stop the wind from gathering speed and racing along.

Wind makes fires hotter and faster-moving, and in winter it sweeps snow into deep drifts. It dries the land by speeding water evaporation, in the same way as a hair dryer works. The wind drops from time to time, but there is always a breeze—it is never entirely still.

In hot countries there is another grassland biome: tropical grassland. Hot weather is not the only difference between tropical and

Grass grows quickly and green in the spring rains, but by midsummer the tops are scorched by the Sun and starved of water, turning to dry, yellow straw.

Climate Change

Grassland boundaries are vague and ever-changing, not fixed lines drawn on a map. In rainy years, young trees take root along the edges of a grassland, and the grassy areas slowly turn into woodland. In dry years, grasses creep back into the wooded areas, which retreat, so the grassland expands. If it is very dry, however, the grasses start to die off, and the grassland becomes desert (right).

In recent decades, climate change as a result of human activities has begun to affect different biomes. Global warming is the gradual warming of the planet as a result of increased levels of greenhouse gases, such as carbon dioxide, in the atmosphere. This increase in carbon dioxide is mainly a result of the burning of fossil fuels, such as coal, oil, and gas. Carbon dioxide is released when these fuels (and almost every other substance) is burned. Other greenhouse gases include methane and ozone. Scientists think there will be more droughts in temperate grasslands, which will make them more like tropical grasslands or deserts. However, the effects of climate change are difficult to predict. Some regions may become wetter, and some may actually become cooler.

temperate grassland—there is also much more rain in the tropics. A temperate grassland gets 250–750 millimeters (10–30 inches) of rain a year, while a tropical grassland can get 1,250 millimeters (50 inches) or more. The hot, wet climate makes tropical grassland a very different place from temperate grassland. The grass grows much faster and taller, and there are many more trees and bushes.

Africa is the best part of the world to compare the two grassland biomes. Vast areas of the continent are covered with savanna—tropical grassland dotted with trees and patches of woodland. Farther south, where it rains less and the winters are considerably cooler, temperate grassland takes over. In southern Africa, the main type of temperate grassland is called veld.

Tornado Alley

Every year, 700 tornadoes sweep across Tornado Alley, a region running from North Dakota and Minnesota to Texas and Louisiana—and some places here are hit three or four times. A tornado is a violently spinning column of air that bursts out of a storm cloud and swoops to the ground. Inside the vortex, air rotates at awesome speeds of up to 800 kilometers per hour (500 mph). Tornadoes are usually born when warm, moist air from the Gulf of Mexico meets cold Canadian air and dry air blowing off the Rockies. The airflows crash into one another with explosive force. Tornadoes can come from any direction, but most travel from southwest to northeast, or west to east.

Tornadoes, or twisters, unleash utter chaos. One of the worst recent outbreaks was in February, 2008, when a series of deadly tornadoes swept through southern United States and the Ohio Valley, killing 57 people and causing more than $1 billion worth of damage. On March 18, 1925, a single mighty twister killed 689 people in Missouri and Illinois.

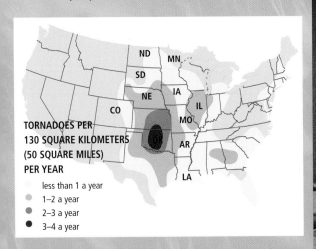

TORNADOES PER
130 SQUARE KILOMETERS
(50 SQUARE MILES)
PER YEAR

less than 1 a year
1–2 a year
2–3 a year
3–4 a year

Endless Variety

Temperate grasslands all share the same basic climate, but each has its own unique conditions. For example, the pampas of South America has milder winters and cooler summers than North America's prairies. Ground frosts are rare in the pampas and deep snow is virtually unheard of.

High ground also gets different weather from lowland regions. The Black Hills of South Dakota and the Ozark Plateau of Missouri are like islands in the prairie. They host a very different mix of plants and animals to the surrounding plains. Here trees such as ponderosa pine and spruce may grow.

Below: Up on the Black Hills of South Dakota, extra moisture allows a unique mix of prairie plants to flourish, including big bluestem grasses and even trees.

White Out

If summers in grasslands can be hot and dry enough to turn the grass to straw, winters can be very severe indeed. Not only is the weather icy cold, but there is usually a thick blanket of snow over much of the land. But this is not the worst of it. Frequently, snowstorms are whipped up into blizzards by the ferocious winds that can tear across the open grassland. When a blizzard occurs, strong winds combine with low temperatures to blow fine, dry snow off the ground, creating an icy maelstrom that cuts visibility to just a few hundred feet and makes movement almost impossible. The worst blizzards can bury animals, cars, and houses—or people venturing outside—in deep drifts of snow. Typically, there are two or three severe

Trails of Fire

Huge grassland fires often break out in late summer and fall. Lightning usually sets them off, but nowadays people also start fires, sometimes by accident and sometimes on purpose. The masses of dead grass stalks burn easily and provide abundant fuel. Winds fan the flames until they are as high as houses, and push the blazing infernos over the dry land. The fires can burn for days, traveling hundreds of miles. Fire is vital to the grasslands. Without fire, tallgrass prairie soon changes to oak-hickory scrub. These fires are a common sight each year on the prairies.

Climographs

Each place in the world has its own pattern of weather. The typical pattern of weather that happens in one place during a year is called climate. We can sum up a place's climate on a climograph, such as the one shown here for St. Louis. The letters along the bottom are the months of the year. The numbers on the left and the small bars show rainfall, and the numbers on the right and the curvy line show temperature. You can see at a glance that St. Louis is hottest in July, but December is the driest month.

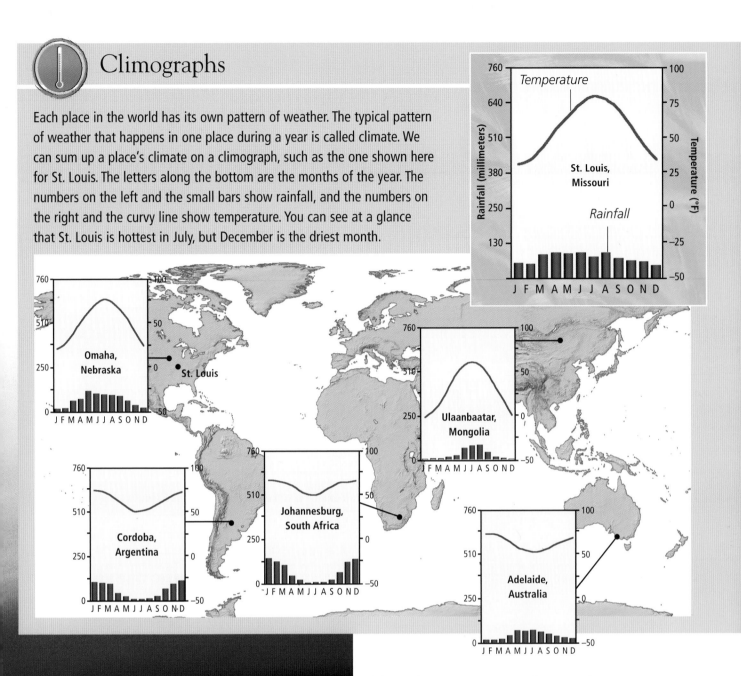

blizzards every winter. They tend to occur when a deep low-pressure system whirls in from the west, gathering power and moisture as it travels eastward. Kansas was hit by severe blizzards in early 2010.

In North America, these low-pressure systems migrate down the east side of the Rocky Mountains and develop into raging blizzards as they move out across the Great Plains. The problem for weather forecasters is that less than one in ten winter lows go on to turn into blizzards. So there is real difficulty in identifying which will turn bad. Many fatalities from blizzards occur because they can strike suddenly, with great severity.

PAMPAS

The pampas grasslands lie at the southern end of South America. They cover a huge flat region between the Andes mountains in the west and the Atlantic Ocean in the east. The weather here on the pampas is generally mild, with pleasantly cool summers.

 Gone Forever

In 1789, huge bones were dug up on a muddy riverbank in the Argentinian pampas. They belonged to a bearlike mammal almost as big as an elephant. This beast had massive, hooked claws, and when it stood on its back legs it would have been 4.5 meters (15 feet) tall. Local people called it the giant mole, but scientists named it *Megatherium*. *Megatherium* may have died out during the last ice age and probably ate leafy branches.

1. Desert Frontiers
In the west, the pampas gradually give way to thorny scrub and dry desert. The Gran Chaco is a large shrubland area on the border between Paraguay and Argentina that marks the northern limit of the pampas. In the northeast, low ground turns to vast marshes in the wet season. This region is called the Pantanal. Farmland fertilizers washed into the marshes threaten wildlife.

2. Andes
The snowcapped peaks of the Andes mountains form a massive barrier to the west of the pampas. Many of the summits rise to 6,100 meters (20,000 feet). They include some of the world's largest volcanoes. Mountain glaciers are shrinking because of global warming.

3. Pampero
A pampero is a cold wind that blows across the pampas, often bringing violent gales and heavy rain. It comes from the icy mountains at the southern tip of South America.

4. Paraná River
The Paraná River flows through the northern pampas. Near the sea, it joins up with the Uruguay River and widens into an enormous estuary called the Río de la Plata. A dam built on the river destroyed a vast area of wilderness. Jaguars are under threat in the region.

5. Palm Savanna
Lines of tall yatay palms crisscross the grassland between the Paraná and Uruguay rivers. They grow up to 18 meters (60 feet) in height.

6. Colorado River
This river marks the southern boundary of the pampas.

7. Ernesto Tornquist National Park
This protected area is one of the last completely natural fragments of pampas grassland in Argentina. Feral horses—mustangs—have an impact on native wildlife here.

8. Campos del Tuyu
In this wildlife preserve on the Argentinian coast, there are many shallow lakes and marshes scattered among the grassland. Flamingos, herons, and other wildfowl live here.

9. Cuchilla Grande
These low, rolling hills in Uruguay aren't very big, but they are still the highest land in the pampas region. Virtually all of the pampas lie only slightly above sea level.

The marshy Salado depression in Argentina's Campos del Tuyu reserve is one of the last refuges of the increasingly rare pampas deer.

La Paz

BOLIVIA

Pantanal

Pacific Ocean

! **1**

Gran Chaco

PARAGUAY

CHILE

ARGENTINA

Asunción

Ojos del
Salado

SOUTH
AMERICA

N

!

2

Andes

!

4

Paraná River

5

Uruguay River

BRAZIL

Lake Mar
Chiquita

3

URUGUAY

Aconcagua

Pampero winds

Fray Bentos

Cuchilla Grande

9

Atlantic

Santiago

Buenos Aires

Ocean

Río de la Plata

Montevideo

Ernesto Tornquist
National Park

! **7**

Campos
del Tuyu

Patagonia

6

Colorado River

8

0   300 miles
0   300   kilometers

Pampas Facts

▲ The word *pampa* comes from a Quechua Indian
word that means "flat surface" or "plain."

▲ The pampas region includes most of northern
Argentina, western Uruguay, and the southernmost
part of Brazil.

▲ Much of the pampas is under threat of being
turned into cattle ranches.

▲ Apart from a few hills, most of the pampas
seems perfectly flat.

GRASSLAND PLANTS

Grasslands are some of the most fertile places on Earth. The grasslands burst with enough plant life to feed amazing numbers of animals.

Temperate grasslands go through a constant process of change. In winter, they look dull brown or gray because the plants are **dormant** (inactive). When spring returns, the welcome rains and rising temperatures breathe new life into the soil. Fresh shoots emerge all over the place, painting the scenery bright green. Masses of flowers add splashes of intense color. As summer wears on, the landscape turns straw-colored. For a brief period in late summer, the grassland is awash with seas of white, yellow, and bluish grass blossoms. When the rains finally dry up, the plants die back, and the land appears drab and lifeless again.

Natural Survivors

To survive such a demanding routine of perpetual change, grassland plants must be exceptionally hardy and adaptable. Grasses fit the bill perfectly. They are natural survivors, the greatest success story of the plant world. They have spread to every continent, even Antarctica, and cover 20 percent of the planet's land surface. There are about 10,000 **species** of grasses,

Kaleidoscope of Colors

In spring, carpets of flowers transform grasslands into a riot of color. In Asian steppes, wild tulips form a mosaic of red and yellow, broken by patches of blue and yellow dwarf irises and scarlet peonies, and a sprinkling of blue sage. In the Texas prairies (below), bluebonnet mixes gloriously with red paintbrush.

Tallgrass prairie was one of North America's wonders, with a profusion of flowers, songbirds, and insects. Now there is little left, as most has become farmland.

all of which share one very special characteristic—a way of growing that allows them to survive being ravaged by fire, drought, or animals.

Back to Basics

Most plants grow outward from the tips of their shoots, twigs, or branches, but grasses grow from the bottom up. This is one of the secrets of their success. Each grass plant sends out new shoots from a special base near the soil or underground.

Growing in this way has many advantages. Out in the open, a blade of grass risks being chewed, ripped, or burned. Such rough treatment would be fatal for ordinary plants. But it is no problem for grass because the really important bits—the growing buds—are safely out of harm's way. This explains why people can keep mowing lawns frequently without killing off the grass.

Below: In the moist conditions of the eastern prairies, tallgrass prairie species such as Indian grass and big bluestem can grow up to 3 meters (10 feet) high.

Tall and Short

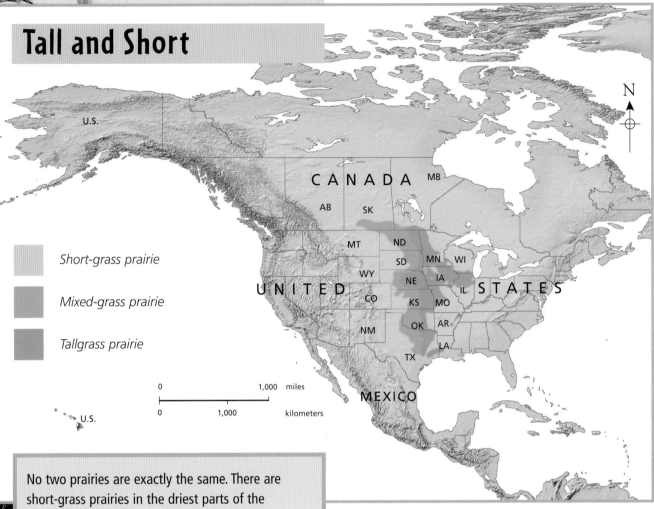

Short-grass prairie

Mixed-grass prairie

Tallgrass prairie

No two prairies are exactly the same. There are short-grass prairies in the driest parts of the Midwest and tallgrass prairies in the wetter areas.

Heavy clouds that move in from the Pacific Ocean dump most of their rain on the western United States and Canada, especially the Rocky Mountains. By the time the clouds have passed the Rockies and reached the Great Plains, they have little water left. This is why the short-grass prairies are in the west in dry states like Montana, Wyoming, and Colorado. These dusty prairies provided the location for many old westerns and for popular TV series such as Bonanza and High Chaparral.

Farther east, it starts to rain harder again, which is why there are tallgrass prairies in eastern Midwest states such as Minnesota, Iowa, and Missouri. Between these two types of prairies lies a halfway zone called mixed prairie. Some central states, such as North and South Dakota, Nebraska, and Kansas, have all three kinds of prairies.

Whenever a grass plant loses one of its blades, it quickly grows back. Nibbling by animals, mowing, and burning actually encourage the grass to grow faster and healthier. It's a bit like having a haircut. Left on its own, grass soon gets straggly and out of control, but regular trimming helps keep it in good shape.

Perfectly Formed

Grasses are the ideal shape for highly exposed places like plains and hillsides. Instead of broad leaves they have thin, flattened blades clustered around tall stems. This is a winning design for lots of reasons. Blades of grass are flexible and bend in the wind without breaking off. If a heavy animal treads on them, they usually spring back. Just as

23

When the spring rains come, grasses like this creeping soft grass (below) are astonishingly quick at growing and putting out seeds to establish new plants.

In the high, dry western plains of Wyoming (above), there are still vast areas of short-grass prairie where buffalo grass and blue grama grass grow.

important, the narrow blades stay cool when the Sun is directly overhead in the middle of the day. At midday in high summer, the Sun's rays are fierce, and temperate grasslands have few bushes or trees to give shade. However, the powerful rays beat straight down at this time so touch only the tip of each grass blade. If grasses had wide, round leaves, they would soon shrivel up and die.

Root of the Matter

We can see only a small part of each grass plant—most of it is hidden beneath the surface. A massive network of roots spreads outward in every direction and pushes a long way into the soil. The roots of some grasses, such as the bluestems found in America's tallgrass prairies, reach 3 meters (10 feet) deep. Deep roots can tap into underground water in times of no rain. Shallow roots soak up surface moisture from brief cloudbursts.

An extra function of roots is to store food. Many grassland plants are equipped with fat, fleshy roots for just this purpose. Sometimes they also have bulky **bulbs** and tubers—even bigger emergency food reserves.

Testing Times

Really dry or cold periods are big problems for grassland plants. Many grasses stop growing entirely, leaving only dead stems and seed heads above ground. When rain falls again or the temperature rises, they burst back into life from their roots. Many of the flowering plants that grow among the grasses rely on a different survival strategy. They die away completely when the going gets tough, but not before scattering enormous quantities of seeds. The seeds can endure parched earth or freezing cold for months or even years on end. When conditions improve at last, the seeds sprout immediately, sending out roots, shoots, and stems to establish brand-new plants.

A Living Carpet

As grass plants grow, they join up with their neighbors to make a carpet, called turf. Below the surface, turf is a crazy mass of tangled roots. Turf is what holds grasslands together.

Without this tightly woven mat of plants, the soil would be too loose. Gales and rain showers would blow and wash it away in no time, leaving a desert.

Wild turf looks totally different from the lawn in a garden or the manicured ground at the local golf course. Gardeners keep their lawns neat, but natural grasslands are very messy by comparison, with many clumps and bumps everywhere.

Turf is a mix of different plants jumbled together. Besides grasses, there are all kinds of sedges, herbs, and flowers. Sedges look similar to grasses but prefer wetter places beside streams or in damp hollows. Many grassland plants grow together in bunches, while others are scattered about here and there. Some plants are tiny and cling to the soil; others are much taller. A few grasses have become giants. In parts of Nepal, strands of grass reach 7.6 meters (25 feet) high.

Sand and Mud

Bare patches of dirt appear in the driest grassland areas. For example, sandhills pop up throughout the short-grass prairies in parts of Colorado, Kansas, and Nebraska. Dry-country plants grow on these dusty little mounds, including spiky yuccas, sagebrush, and prickly

Windblown Wanderers

Tumbleweeds make use of the wind to spread their seeds. In the summer heat, tumbleweeds dry out and die, turning into prickly balls. Strong autumnal winds easily pick them up and send them hurtling across the landscape. As the dead tumbleweeds bounce along, they scatter thousands of seeds. There are many kinds of tumbleweeds on the North American prairies, especially in the west.

Each area of grassland has its own unique range of plants. Here in the dry Western Australian bush, tussocks of spinifex grass mingle with mulga bushes.

pear cacti. Yuccas have tough, waxy leaves to stop them from losing moisture. At the other extreme, heavy rains swamp huge areas of pampas in spring. Marsh-loving plants thrive in the muddy ground. The eastern pampas are the lushest of temperate grasslands.

Lots of Layers

Up close, a wild grassland is like a miniature forest. If you go to a meadow, prairie, or wasteland and get down on your hands and knees, you'll find the plants form several layers. Tall grasses and flowers hide lots of smaller grasses, herbs, mosses, and lichens that are growing underneath. These dwarf plants flourish in a **microclimate** down near the ground, protected from the worst weather by the taller plants. It's a hidden world,

Soil Matters

The soil in temperate grasslands is tremendously fertile. Its vital ingredient is an organic material called humus, which forms when plants and animals die and their bodies decompose (rot away). Temperate grasslands have much deeper, richer soil than tropical grasslands or rain forests. The cooler conditions slow the process of decomposition, allowing an extra-thick layer of humus to build up. The interlinked maze of grass roots holds all this goodness, and moisture, in place. You can tell how rich soil is from its color. The darker the soil, the more fertile it is. In the most fertile grasslands of all, such as the prairies of eastern Nebraska, the earth is jet-black. Elsewhere, the color of the ground varies from chestnut to pale brown, as in the northernmost prairies. Savannas and other tropical grasslands have thinner, reddish or yellowish soils.

All About Grass

In any grassland, no matter how small, you should be able to find several kinds of grasses. Many grasslands have dozens of varieties. Some of them are highly distinctive—prairie needlegrass is sharp enough to pierce clothing. But it is true that the great majority look pretty similar. Usually a few species are far more plentiful than the rest, and this is one of the ways biologists sort grasslands into different categories.

Animals can be very fussy eaters. Sometimes they depend on just one or two types of plants, ignoring all the others. In many of the Midwest's short-grass prairies, the main species is buffalo grass, which has curly, bluish-green blades. As its name suggests, buffalo grass was the favorite food of the huge herds of buffalo—or to give them their correct name, bison—that once roamed the Great Plains. Most grasses may look the same to us, but bison obviously know the difference.

Nature's Medicine Store

For generations, Native Americans have used natural remedies prepared from prairie plants to help treat a variety of illnesses. They used extracts taken from coneflowers, or echinacea, to help fight colds and flu. Some people think that these plant drugs work by stimulating the human immune system. There are nine species of coneflowers. In late spring and summer they produce a cone-shaped mass of tiny petals, surrounded by a ring of larger purple, pink, yellow, or white petals.

swarming with billions of insects and other small animals. Turf is truly the pulsing heart of the temperate grassland biome.

Larger bushes and trees get only a foothold in the most sheltered spots. Wherever rivers or streams carve shallow valleys into the prairies, ribbons of cottonwoods, willows, and oaks line the banks. In the southern African veld, thickets of thorny shrubs and flat-topped acacia trees grow in stony valleys and on the sides of small rocky outcrops. These features give protection from the region's wildfires and winter frosts. However, the weather conditions are still too severe for normal forest to develop.

Remarkable Trees

Not all grasslands are treeless. The dry, grass-covered plains of southern Australia are studded with certain kinds of eucalyptus trees (gum trees). These are special because they can thrive in virtual deserts and survive bush fires. Their bark is thick enough to resist flames. The searing heat of a bush fire causes a chemical reaction inside the trees, which triggers new growth. Soon, there are

Grassland flowers like Texas bluebonnet have to bloom quickly in spring to reproduce before they are swamped by the rapidly growing grass.

Shaped by Fire

Although grassland fires can be ferocious, they are essential to the health of the biome. Heaps of dead plant material go up in flames, clearing the way for new growth next year. The blazes also release vital nutrients trapped inside the old debris, pumping up the fertility level of the soil.

Grassland plants have many features that help them cope with even the fiercest fires. Their deep roots and often their low-level buds remain unscathed, and their fireproof seeds can survive being roasted. Once the ashes cool, it is only a week or two before the first shoots begin to reappear. Drawing on the reserves in their fleshy roots, the grasses soon spread to take advantage of the open ground and newly enriched soil. Trees are often not so lucky. They grow more slowly than grasses so barely have time to recover from one

scorching before the next blaze breaks out. And unless they are tall enough to keep their growing tips out of the flames' reach, they suffer the full force of the fire.

green shoots sprouting all over the scorched trunks, repairing the damage. The white-hot temperatures also make the eucalyptus seeds split open and fall to the ground, ready to start growing into new trees as soon as there is enough moisture.

Turf Wars

Every grassland is a battlefield, although the struggle taking place is invisible to human eyes. Plants never stop competing with one another to get the most sunlight and water. Those that win the fight for resources grow bigger and crowd out the losers, which may wither away. It is a race against time.

Grassland plants can't afford to wait around—they rush to make full use of the spring rains before the summer dry season arrives. On the prairies and steppes, some flowers appear even before the winter snow has finished melting. Many of the world's fastest growing plants are types of grass, including the fastest of all—bamboo.

Almost all modern wheat plants are descended from two wild grasses—einkorn and wild goat grass—that grew in southwest Asia thousands of years ago.

Most grassland plants have another trick. By releasing vast amounts of seeds, they make sure they are first to take over patches of bare ground. When ground is cleared, grassland plants are the first to colonize.

Flower Power

Grasslands contain far more flowers than most biomes. Surprising though it may seem, grasses and weeds are flowering plants themselves, though their flowers are small and inconspicuous—a far cry from the flamboyant colors of roses or orchids. Most grass flowers are pale, feathery spikes—not always easy to see amid the sea of green blades and stems.

Edible Grass

Vast areas of grassland are covered by a cultivated grass—wheat. Wheat is an annual grass plant, with a head containing 50–75 kernels, or seeds, which are ground to make flour, or sown to grow a new crop. The seed begins to grow once there is enough moisture in the soil. In spring, the plant sprouts many green leaves (below) and 20 or so golden flowers or spikes. As it ripens through summer, the whole plant turns golden.

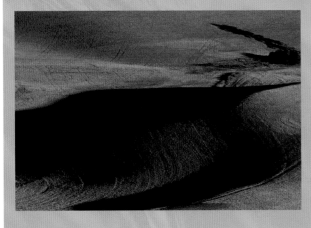

Flowers play a crucial role in a plant's life cycle. They enable the plant to reproduce sexually. Unlike animals, plants can't move around to find mates, so they need other ways to bring their male and female sex cells together. The solution is to make pollen—a dustlike substance that carries male sex cells. Most flowers have both male and female parts. The male parts make pollen; the female parts have a sticky surface to capture pollen. When a grain of pollen lands on the female part of a flower, it sprouts and grows downward into the flower, delivering the male cell to a female sex cell. The two cells then join, and a seed forms around them.

Grassland plants have lots of ways of transferring their pollen between each other. Plants with colorful flowers use insects such as bees and butterflies. To attract the insects, they produce bright blooms or strong perfumes. When an insect lands on a flower, it gets dusted with pollen, which rubs off on the next flower it visits. It won't do the job for nothing, so as a reward, every flower it goes to offers it an energy-boosting drink of sugary nectar.

On the Wind

There's no need for grass flowers to be impressive because they don't have to tempt insects to visit them. Grasses use another technique to spread their pollen to other grass plants—the wind. However, wind is less efficient than insects because it blows most of the pollen away. To compensate, grass flowers produce masses of very fine pollen so at least some will land on other plants.

Grassland winds are strong and reliable, which is perfect for pollination. When the wind blows a spike of grass flowers, clouds of microscopic pollen grains fly into the air. Virtually all of them degrade within a day, but just enough pollen reaches waiting grass flowers in the surrounding area.

VELD

The veld is a very particular type of grassland that carpets the mountainsides and high plateaus of southeast Africa. This grassland supports a wealth of rare wildlife.

AFRICA

Okavango delta

● Windhoek

NAMIBIA

1 (!)

Kalahari Desert

12

SOUTH AFRICA

Cape Town
Table Mountain ▲●

1. Kalahari Desert
One of the world's biggest deserts lies to the west of the veld. Although a desert, the Kalahari has vast areas of dry grassland and is home to large herds of zebras and antelope, such as gemsboks, elands, and wildebeest. Scientists fear the Kalahari will increase in size because of global warming.

2. Vaal River
By the Vaal River lies the Vaalbos, a reserve saved from diamond mines near Kimberley. The reserve is now home to black rhino, white rhino, buffalo, eland, and hartebeests. But the area's precious wetlands are now threatened by mining,

which causes habitat loss for wildlife and river pollution.

3. Tswaing Crater
Some 200,000 years ago, a meteorite crashed into the veld to create a circular crater 1.1 kilometers (0.67 miles) across.

4. Limpopo River
To the north of the veld, the land drops to the floodplain of the Limpopo. This area is a refuge for 34 species of frogs, such as the sandveld pyxie, and 116 species of reptiles, including crocodiles and such rarities as the De Coster's spade-snouted worm lizard. In the river live almost 50 species of fish, including lungfish.

Some 150 years ago, vast herds of antelope called blesboks roamed the veld grasslands, but hunters took their toll, and now only small numbers survive.

Veld Facts

▲ The word *veld* means "field" in the Afrikaans language of South Africa.

▲ There are several different kinds of veld including high veld (high plateaus), low veld (bush-clad lowland plains), thorn veld, and grass veld.

▲ The bushveld found over much of northern South Africa is a kind of veld, with a mix of tall grasses and trees such as acacia thorns and baobabs.

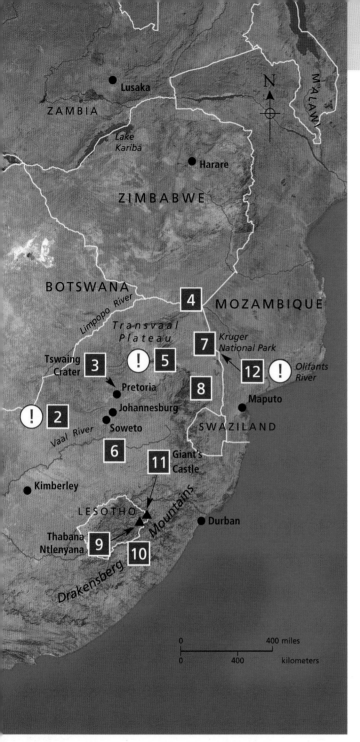

0 | 400 miles
0 | 400 kilometers

5. Transvaal Plateau
Transvaal's high veld is a grassy, upland plateau between the Limpopo and Vaal rivers, mostly 1,220–1,800 meters (4,000–6,000 feet) above sea level. Scientists predict that global warming will make the plateau drier.

6. Kopjes
A kopje is a small rocky outcrop. Thousands of kopjes are dotted across the veld. They are important refuges for a variety of animals, including tiny klipspringer antelope and rock hyraxes (which look a bit like woodchucks, but are distantly related to elephants).

7. Kruger National Park
One of the oldest national parks, Kruger preserves a mix of veld and woodland. It is a vital reserve in the conservation of elephants and a key refuge for about 350 African hunting dogs. It is also home to 146 other mammal species, including 90,000 impalas, 17,000 zebras, and 9,600 wildebeests.

8. Kloofs
Kloofs are steep valleys that slice through the veld. Thickets of thorny bushes and trees grow on their slopes.

9. Thabana Ntlenyana
At 3,482 meters (11,425 feet) tall, this mountain is the highest in the Drakensberg range—and all of southern Africa.

10. Drakensberg Mountains
This chain of rocky mountains marks the eastern edge of the veld. It snakes along for 1,000 kilometers (625 miles).

11. Giant's Castle
Formed from volcanic rock, Giant's Castle is a spectacular jagged ridge in Lesotho.

12. Olifants River
This river crosses Kruger National Park. During the dry season, it is a magnet for the park's thirsty animals. In 2008, many crocodiles in the river died from the effects of mining pollutants.

Earth Pig

The aardvark is one of the veld's strangest-looking residents. It is about the size of a pig, with large, pink ears like a donkey's. It uses its powerful claws to smash open ant and termite nests, then pokes in its long, sticky tongue to pull out the insects. The aardvark is an expert burrower and can dig a hole for itself with astonishing speed. Aardvark holes can be so big that people fall into them, and they are a serious hazard to vehicles. The word aardvark is Dutch for "earth pig."

33

GRASSLAND ANIMALS

Life in a temperate grassland is a real endurance test for animals. But for those that can survive the harsh climate and keep enemies at bay, there are rich pickings to be found.

In a grassland, all the usual hiding places such as bushes, trees, dense undergrowth, fallen timber, or rock piles are in short supply. An obvious solution is to create your own hiding place—a burrow. Temperate grasslands are home to far more burrowing animals than any other of the world's biomes.

Half of all the mammals found on steppes live in burrows of one sort or another, compared to just 5 percent of forest mammals. They include dozens of different small rodents, such as mice, voles, hamsters, and gerbils, as well as larger species such as marmots. Their secret world of tunnels and passages adds a whole extra dimension to the featureless landscape above.

Digging the Dirt

The simplest shelters are just hollows in the ground, which rabbits, hares, and ground-living birds such as quails and partridges scrape out in no time. These give temporary protection until the danger has passed. But many animals dig down much farther

Above: With their unusually long legs, burrowing owls are well-equipped for peering over short-grass prairie and scurrying after prey.

Left: A mole's bite contains enough venom to paralyze an earthworm. When the hunting is good, moles make stashes of worms for eating later—still alive.

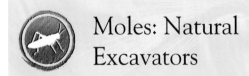

Moles: Natural Excavators

Moles are extremely common in prairies and steppes, though seldom seen—they rarely leave their tunnel networks and move to deeper tunnels in cold or very dry weather. They constantly repair and extend their tunnels, shunting the waste soil up to the surface as molehills. Moles are incredibly efficient digging machines, with broad, spadelike forefeet attached to massive shoulder muscles. Their short, supersoft fur helps them slip through their tunnels without getting stuck. Moles have poor eyesight but a good sense of smell. They feel around with their delicate, naked snouts to locate earthworms and other prey.

to make complex underground homes. Grassland soil is perfect for digging in. Because of the dense mat of tangled roots, it rarely caves in, unlike loose earth or sand.

A life spent digging requires lots of **adaptations**. Burrowing mammals have muscular legs with long, strong claws for excavating. Their bodies are compact for moving down twisting tunnels and squeezing past awkward roots and stones. They need special eyelids that stop flying dirt from getting in, although hearing and smell are far more important than vision in pitch-black tunnels. The pocket gophers of North America even have lips behind their front teeth that stop them from swallowing soil. Most burrowing mammals also have sensitive whiskers on the front of their head. Twitching constantly, the whiskers feel the tunnel walls to pick up faint vibrations made by the movement of other animals. The vibrations tell the burrowers what is going on around them, like messages traveling along telephone wires.

Trading Places

Animals that can't dig their own burrows often take over the old ones of other species. Many grassland snakes do this, including several of the ratsnake and rattlesnake species found on the prairies.

The burrowing owl moves into burrows, too, because there are no trees to nest in. It lives throughout much of the Americas, from the prairies to the pampas of Argentina. In its North American range, the burrowing owl likes to nest in the old burrows of prairie dogs and badgers. Burrowing owls are unusual among owls not only because they live in grasslands rather than forests and nest underground, but also because they are often active during the day. They can sometimes be seen watching for prey in broad daylight.

Secret Cities

Black-tailed prairie dogs (left) are a kind of ground squirrel that live on the Great Plains in colonies, or "towns," containing many thousands of animals. Each town is a huge burrow up to 5 meters (16 feet) deep that often extends for thousands of square meters. The underground maze includes many entrances, sleeping chambers, and breeding dens. Prairie dogs play a key role in the wildlife of the prairies, and more than 200 other kinds of creatures make their homes near their colonies. The burrows are so big that many other animals live inside them, from cottontail rabbits (right) to prairie rattlesnakes (below).

Taking Cover

Going underground allows animals to escape not only their **predators** but also the worst of the weather. Burrows offer protection from driving winds, sudden storms, grass fires, scorching summers, and freezing winters. They are cooler than outside in summer, and warmer than outside in winter. Many grassland animals avoid the midsummer heat by spending the day in their burrows and emerging only at night. Lots of grasslands come alive in the dark after being really quiet during the day.

Large mammals that must spend all their lives out in the open cope with harsh weather in other ways. North American bison (buffalo) have shaggy, windproof fur, and in winter they grow a much heavier coat with an especially thick mane. Herds of bison tend to huddle together for warmth in winter, keeping the younger calves snug in the middle, well out of the wind.

Protected against the cold by their shaggy coats, bison find grass to eat in winter by swinging their great heads from side to side to clear the snow.

Deep Sleep

Rodents, tortoises, snakes, and lizards survive wintry weather by entering a deep sleeplike state called **hibernation**. In fall, animals with burrows retreat there, while the rest, such as tortoises, simply bury themselves. The body temperature of hibernating animals plunges, and their breathing and **metabolism** (body chemistry) slow down considerably.

The thirteen-lined ground squirrel is a good example of an animal that hibernates. Safe inside its winter den, the squirrel lowers

On the surface, the prairies may seem almost lifeless in winter, but below ground, millions of creatures, from rodents to rattlesnakes, are biding their time until spring.

Saiga Under Threat

The saiga is an antelope that lives on the steppes. It has a long, flexible nose, which it uses to warm the cold air it inhales in winter and also to prevent itself from breathing in dust in summer. In the early 20th century, the saiga became almost extinct, but its numbers bounced back to more than a million by 1950. However, in recent years it has become a target for poachers because there is a demand for its horns in traditional Chinese medicine. Only male saiga grow horns, so most of the saiga left today are herds of females with too few males to father calves. Today, there are about 50,000 of this critically endangered animal, mainly in Kazakhstan, Mongolia, and Kalmykia (part of the Russian Federation), which is raising awareness of this antelope's plight by declaring 2010 the "Year of the Saiga."

In spring, bobolinks arrive in the North American prairie from their wintering grounds far south in Argentina. The males fill the air with their bubbling mating calls.

Sleepy Summers

Amphibians become inactive in summer. If they stayed active, the hot, dry weather might dry out their moist skin and kill them. For this reason, many grassland frogs and toads retreat to hiding places and spend the summer in a kind of suspended animation. This summer equivalent of hibernation is called **estivation**.

Frogs and toads enter this special resting state whenever their pools or creeks dry up. They hide in dense tangles of turf or wriggle into the ground. Spadefoot toads use ridges on their back feet as shovels, and once below ground they shed several layers of skin to make a watertight cocoon around themselves. When rain falls, the toads break out. African bullfrogs are much fatter and may wait under the veld for several years if necessary.

The Power of Flight

Birds can fly long distances in search of food and shelter—a huge advantage in temperate grasslands. Small perching birds such as larks, pipits, buntings, sparrows, and finches feed on insects and seeds, which quickly become scarce as winter sets in. As a result, the birds gather in flocks and fly for miles, giving them more chance of finding new food supplies, with many eyes scanning the ground.

its body temperature from 35°C (95°F) to around 2.7°C (37°F)—barely above freezing point. It breathes just once every five minutes, and its heartbeat slows to only a few beats per minute.

Grassland animals use far less energy when they hibernate, allowing them to spend long periods without eating or drinking. They stay alive by slowly using fat reserves built up during the spring and summer. Reptiles sleep all winter without a break, while mammals often wake up at regular intervals to feed. Many of them, including hamsters and pocket gophers, store large quantities of food in their burrows to snack on through the winter. The regular wake-ups are thought to be vital for keeping the animal's immune system working well and disease at bay.

Food from the Flames

When a serious grass fire breaks out, most animals flee for their lives. But several kinds of birds take advantage of the confusion and panic. As the advancing flames force masses of insects, small mammals, and snakes to abandon their hiding places, flocks of swallows, martins, hawks, and storks arrive to grab an easy meal.

Most people think parrots live only in tropical forests, but several brightly colored species make their homes in the plains of southeastern Australia. They include small, long-tailed parakeets and cockatiels, and crow-sized cockatoos. During the day, small groups of these grassland parrots spread out to search the open country for seeds. In the evening, the groups assemble noisily into much larger flocks to visit water holes and roost together in eucalyptus trees.

Many grassland birds undertake longer journeys, or **migrations**, to escape winter food shortages. This is especially true of prairie and steppe birds. For example, the bobolink breeds in the northern prairies but spends winter in the Argentinian pampas. To get there it must fly south to the southern states, cross the Gulf of Mexico, and then travel the length of South America. In spring, it flies all the way back to raise a family. Migratory birds that breed in the Asian steppes spend the winter in Africa or India.

Harris's hawk catches prey by watching patiently from a low perch, then swooping silently over the grass to grab its victim in its talons.

Light Show

On warm summer nights, tiny lights flicker on and off all over many damp grasslands. They belong to lightning bugs, or fireflies, which are trying to attract a mate. The flashes are a code that indicates the bugs' species, sex, and readiness to mate. The light is given off by a chemical reaction inside the abdomen (the rear body section of insects).

Hide-and-Seek

In open country, predators can spot their prey from a long way off. This forces grassland animals to keep a low profile—no wonder grasslands often seem like empty places where nothing much happens.

Small animals try to stay out of sight inside the forest of grass stalks. Eventually, the endless comings and goings of mice, voles, rats, and other small rodents create hidden pathways through the turf. All kinds of animals use these paths to commute between their burrows and feeding areas. However, they are up against predators with extremely acute senses. Birds of prey have razor-sharp

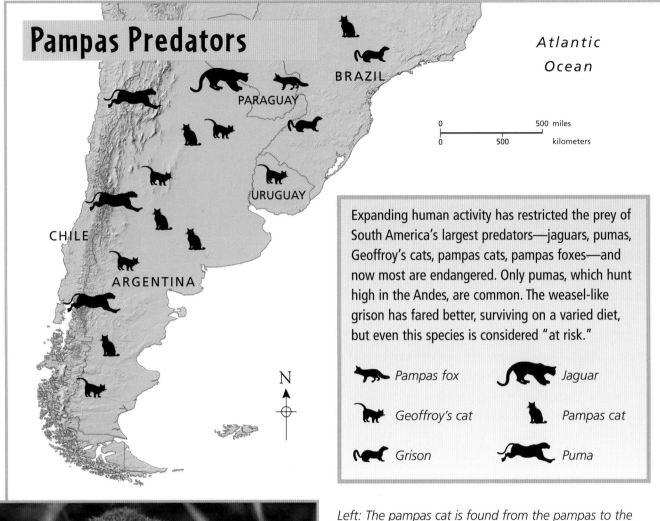

Pampas Predators

BRAZIL

Atlantic Ocean

PARAGUAY

CHILE

URUGUAY

ARGENTINA

0   500   miles
0   500   kilometers

Expanding human activity has restricted the prey of South America's largest predators—jaguars, pumas, Geoffroy's cats, pampas cats, pampas foxes—and now most are endangered. Only pumas, which hunt high in the Andes, are common. The weasel-like grison has fared better, surviving on a varied diet, but even this species is considered "at risk."

Pampas fox   Jaguar

Geoffroy's cat   Pampas cat

Grison   Puma

N

Left: The pampas cat is found from the pampas to the savanna regions of Brazil called cerrado. It hunts mostly at night, catching small mammals, birds, and reptiles.

vision for spotting tiny movements in the grass far below. Eagles and hawks soar high in the air to scan for prey, while harriers hunt by gliding silently just above the grass. Snakes are often the most common predators in grasslands. Many are rodent killers. They hunt by using a flick of the tongue to taste the air for a prey's scent. Up close, some snakes can also sense infrared (heat) and "see" an animal's body heat through the grass. Burrows are not always safe havens from snakes. On the prairies, for example, kingsnakes and corn snakes often slide quietly into rodent burrows to go hunting.

Most large hunters in temperate grasslands belong to the dog family. Among them are the coyote and swift fox of North America, the jackals of Africa, and the Australian dingo. All dogs have excellent senses of smell and hearing. They usually detect their prey before catching sight of it.

A big proportion of the coyote's diet consists of small animals like mice. Its favorite technique for catching them is to advance slowly through the grass, pausing regularly to watch and listen. When the coyote pinpoints its target, it leaps straight up into the air, then drops on top of the victim.

The Great Escape

Being able to move fast can mean the difference between life or death for many grassland animals. Some species, such as the eastern cottontail rabbit of North America, make a dash for the nearest available cover. Others, including the black-tailed jackrabbit, have the strength to run a long way until predators give up the chase. Really fast species like jackrabbits can live in more open habitats with shorter grass.

Coyotes are among the most adaptable of predators, eating anything from pronghorns to garbage. In winter they catch mice in the snow with a sudden pounce.

Speed is so important that you see some strange-looking animals in temperate grasslands. The Australian emu and the rhea of South America are giant, long-legged birds that can run faster than a person. They are far too big and heavy to fly. The springhare of the African veld looks like a cross between a kangaroo and a rabbit. It has chunky back legs that allow it to leap forward up to 2 meters (6.5 feet) with one bound.

A number of other grassland rodents also have enormous back legs for making quick getaways, including the gerbils of central Asia, the rat kangaroos of Australia, and the kangaroo rats and mice of North America. All these creatures also use their back legs for excavating burrows and for scrabbling around for seeds. Males drum on the ground with their hefty legs to produce a mating call. Although all these animals look alike and behave in similar ways, they live thousands of miles apart and are not closely related to one another. The Australian rat kangaroos may look ratlike, but in fact they are small kangaroos, not rodents. They have evolved along the same lines because they live in similar habitats, a process scientists call **convergent evolution**.

Record Breakers

Pronghorn antelope are easily the fastest mammals on the prairies. Their name is misleading because they are not real antelope but relatives of wild goats. Unlike goats, however, pronghorns are built for speed.

Pronghorn antelope have phenomenal stamina. They can run nonstop for up to 24 kilometers (15 miles) at an average speed of around 56 kilometers (35 miles) per hour. To put this feat in perspective, the world's fastest sprinter can reach almost 37 kilometers (23 miles) per hour for barely ten seconds before having to slow down. Even 2-week-old baby pronghorns are able to race along at tremendous speed, which is just as well because they are a favorite prey of coyotes, wolves, and pumas.

Sticking Together

Many large grassland animals live in herds. It pays to stick together because predators then find it much harder to catch the animals by surprise—with so many eyes and ears on the lookout, an approaching predator is soon spotted. And when all the members of a herd are running along together, it is difficult for a hunter to select an individual and keep track.

Antelope, deer, horses, and bison all live in herds. So does the blesbok, a reddish brown antelope with white "stockings" that lives on the veld of Africa. Until the 18th century, blesboks gathered in herds of many thousands, but human hunters killed most of them. The same happened to the bison and pronghorn antelope of North America.

Playing Defensive

Only a few grassland animals stand their ground when threatened, because it is such a risky thing to do. At night, the crested porcupine leaves its burrow in the veld to feed on roots and fruits. Its black-and-white spines are longer and sharper than those of its distant North American relative. The spines usually frighten off even big carnivores such as leopards and brown hyenas. As a last resort, the porcupine charges backward at its enemies and tries to stab them with heavy-duty spines called quills.

The African leopard tortoise is equally tough for predators to deal with. It simply retreats inside its hard shell if it is attacked. If a predator picks up a tortoise, it finds the tortoise hard to crush due to the shell's high, domed shape.

Hungry Hordes

The reason grasslands are able to support such impressive numbers of animals is simple. There is plenty to eat. Grass is packed with nutrients and soon grows back when grazed. It tastes awful to us, and we have not evolved the ability to digest it. However, grazers (animals that eat grass) have very different stomachs from humans. Microorganisms that live inside their stomachs and intestines help them convert the grass into sugar.

Grazing mammals such as antelope and bison—and today vast numbers of livestock such as cattle and sheep—are the most obvious grass eaters, but they are not alone. Grassland plants are also attacked by vast armies of invertebrates (animals without backbones), including ants, termites, beetles, grasshoppers, and snails. The larvae (grubs) of many flies, butterflies, and moths also feed on grassland plants. Together, these tiny animals eat more grassland plants than all the large grazers combined.

Termites have a particularly big impact on grasslands. They use their strong mouthparts to shear off grass stems. Then they carry the small pieces to their nests to feed the grubs. Some termites dig nests underground, but others build mounds on the surface from thousands of mouthfuls of soil stuck together with saliva. They soon harden under the Sun to become rock-solid castles.

Wonderful Worms

The rich soil of temperate grasslands crawls with countless numbers of earthworms. They are vital to the health of the biome. Every earthworm spends its entire life burrowing through the soil. It sucks soil into its mouth, located right at the front, and digests the

Marvelous Manure

Dung can tell us a surprising amount about the animal that left it. Bison produce soft dung that crumbles into a fine powder. This shows that bison have a highly effective digestive system that can squeeze all the goodness out of the grass they eat. Horse dung is harder and lumpy, with bits of grass stalks in it—horses are less efficient at digesting grass than bison. Traditionally, Native Americans and European settlers in North America burned dung as a fuel for cooking and keeping warm.

minute particles of rotting plant matter as the soil passes through its body. Then it squirts the waste soil out of its rear end. Worms move so much earth around that their activities improve the soil. Their hard work allows in more air and churns up all the nutrients, just like the plows and spades of farmers and gardeners.

Horses' ancestors were short-legged woodland animals, and they only evolved into fast-running, long-legged animals as climates changed and grasslands spread.

STEPPES

Stretching right across the heart of Asia is a vast belt of desolate, windswept grasslands—the steppes. They form one of the last great wilderness areas in the world.

 ## Steppe Facts

▲ The steppe region extends from Ukraine and Russia in eastern Europe, through southern Siberia and Kazakhstan, all the way to Mongolia and northern China. The southernmost steppes reach as far south as Turkey, Iran, and Iraq.

▲ The steppes stretch almost a third of the way around the world.

▲ Most of the steppes are uninhabited. Despite being a vast country, Mongolia's population is only 2.5 million—that's smaller than several U.S. cities.

▲ In Mongolia, horse-racing is a children's sport. Most champion jockeys retire by the time they reach their teens.

1. Kirghiz Steppe
The Kirghiz Steppe is an immense grassy plain reaching from the Caspian Sea east to the Altai Mountains. This is the world's largest area of dry steppe, home to the endangered saiga antelope. Other residents include marmots, pikas, and corsac foxes, as well as many birds, such as pallid harriers.

2. Zhezkazgan
The Russian space program has its headquarters here in central Kazakhstan, south of the Kazakh capital of Astana.

3. Astana
The capital of Kazakhstan, once known as Akmola.

4. Lake Balkhash
One of the few large areas of water in the dry Kazakh steppes, Lake Balkhash is home to a unique range of fish, including wild carp and perch. Overfishing and pollution have resulted in the extinction of certain fish.

5. Nayramdal Uur
On the Kazakhstan–Mongolia border, this peak is one of the highest in the Altai range, at 4,374 meters (14,350 feet).

In spring, the snow melts and the warm sunshine brings a profusion of wildflowers into bloom on the steppes, including vivid patches of red tulips.

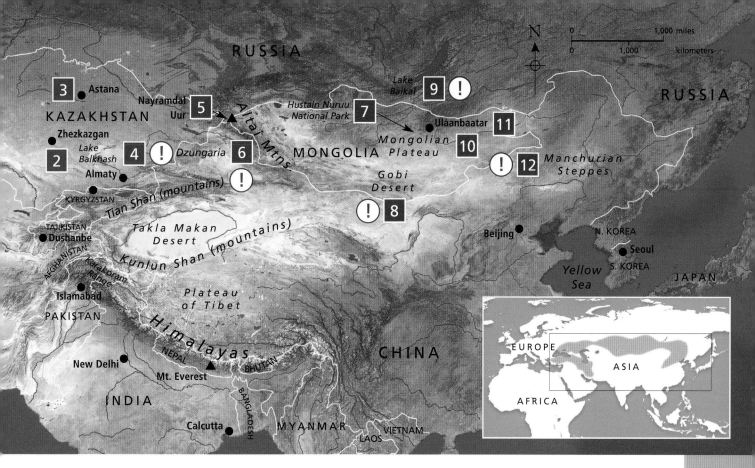

6. Altai Mountains

The Altai Mountains stretch for more than 1,920 kilometers (1,200 miles) from Siberia to the edge of the Gobi Desert and have peaks rising to more than 4,260 meters (14,000 feet). Many of the rivers of the eastern steppes flow from these mountains. Glaciers in the mountains are shrinking because of global warming.

7. Hustain Nuruu National Park

Hunting and herding cattle are banned in this reserve to the south of Ulaanbaatar, which has a small population of Przewalski's wild horses, introduced in the 1990s.

8. Gobi Desert

This wasteland of sand and gravel, sandwiched between the grassy steppes of Mongolia and the highlands of Tibet, is home to the Bactrian camel. In 2007, there were fewer than 1,000 wild Bactrian camels.

9. Lake Baikal

Lake Baikal in Siberia is the world's oldest lake, formed over 25 million years ago as water collected in a deep crack in Earth's surface. It is also the world's deepest lake—more than 1.6 kilometers (1 mile) deep—containing a fifth of the world's freshwater. Its long isolation from the rest of the world means a unique range of creatures has evolved there, including the coregone fish and the Baikal seal, the world's only freshwater seal. Pollution is a growing problem in the lake.

10. Mongolian Plateau

Large parts of Mongolia lie above 1,980 meters (6,500 feet). Farther west, the steppes are much lower and flatter.

11. Ulaanbaatar

Mongolia's capital is highly industrialized, and its factories provide one of the region's few sources of employment other than herding cattle.

12. Manchurian Steppes

The vast Manchurian steppes are roamed by huge herds of Mongolian gazelles. Spread around the steppes are also extensive marshes and reed beds where gigantic flocks of oriental storks and demoiselle cranes breed. Overgrazing by livestock is turning areas of the steppes into desert.

The Original Horse

Most so-called "wild" horses, including the mustang of North America, are descendants of escaped domestic horses. But on the steppes of Mongolia, until quite recently, lived the only truly wild horse —Przewalski's horse. This horse is stockier and has shorter legs than domestic horses. It was first identified by Russian explorer Nicolai Przewalski in the 1880s. The last one was seen in the wild in 1969, but more than 1,000 survived in zoos. In the 1990s, a handful were reintroduced into the wild in Mongolia. By 2004, their numbers had grown to 250.

PEOPLE AND GRASSLANDS

People have raised crops and livestock in temperate grasslands for thousands of years, but the biome can be just as tough for us to survive in as for animals.

The earliest farmers lived in temperate grasslands. About 12,000 years ago, people began to settle down and establish small villages in the southern steppes, in the area that is now Turkey, Iran, and Iraq. They grew cereal crops such as barley, oats, rye, and wheat. Cereals are cultivated (farmed) grasses—relatives of the many wild grasses that flourish throughout the temperate grassland biome. All today's wheat varieties are descended from two kinds of wild grass—einkorn and wild goat grass. People discovered that the seeds of grasses like these make nutritious foods that give us lots of energy. They learned how to grind wheat into flour for cooking and baking bread.

Life of Toil

Before the arrival of tractors and harvesting machines, people had to harvest wheat by hand. Farmers still work this way in some places, including parts of the African veld and parts of the Russian Federation. First the farmers beat the grain (seeds) from the plants. Then they throw basketfuls of grain into the air so that the wind blows away the light husks. The heavier grain falls onto sheets or wooden boards laid on the ground.

Next the farmers pound the grain until it turns into flour. Doing this by hand is back-breaking work, but people long ago discovered a much easier way of making flour. They harnessed the power of the wind or rivers in windmills and waterwheels to grind wheat between revolving stone wheels. The world's oldest stone windmills, which lie in ruins in Iraq and Syria, are around 1,400 years old. Water mills date back even further and were in widespread use in Roman times. The first record of a water mill is from Cabeira in Turkey in 120 B.C.E.

Cowboys

The great days of the American cowboy lasted for just 40 years, from the 1860s to around 1900. Cowboys were superbly skilled at rounding up cattle on the unfenced ranches of the American West. A team of just eight cowboys could control a herd of 2,500 cattle and drive them to market. The cowboys' life was simple and hard. They traveled light and often owned nothing more than their horses, saddles, bedrolls, and the clothes they wore. On the pampas of South America, cowboys are known as gauchos. Like their North American counterparts, the gauchos became folklore heroes and are celebrated in many stories and songs. Even today, gauchos wear the traditional high boots, baggy pants, and felt hats.

Feeding the World

Farming has spread to almost every corner of the temperate grassland biome. Today, grasslands contain a large proportion of the world's best pasture and cropland, and farmers now grow many crops beside wheat, including vegetables, soybeans, and corn. Not all areas of temperate grassland are suitable for raising crops, because the weather can be too extreme. In the west of the Great Plains, for example, it is too dry for wheat and corn, so farmers raise cattle and sheep instead. Cattle ranches, or *estancias*, take up nearly all of the pampas in Argentina and Uruguay.

Many grassland farms and ranches are vast, covering hundreds of square kilometers. They couldn't be managed without an army of

Vast areas of natural grassland have been turned into wheat fields, providing most of the world's basic sustenance, often with two harvests a year.

machines. Teams of workers and combine harvesters work around the clock to bring in the harvest. In the United States, wheat and corn ripen earliest in the south, so the teams start there and move northward as the crops ripen. Railroads and long-distance highways take the farm produce to distant cities. For example, many American beef cattle go to Chicago, Illinois, and Fort Worth, Texas, for processing into fresh meat. Agriculture like this is big business. The largest farms on the prairies, pampas, and rangeland belong to major corporations.

Taming Horses

Stone Age cave paintings show how horses were once hunted for meat. Around 6,000 years ago, nomads on the steppes by the Caspian Sea began to round them up in herds, and in time, began to use them as draft animals (right) and for pulling plows and later chariots. About 3,500 years ago, people in northern Persia learned to ride.

All the world's horses are descended from the wild horses that roamed the steppes. There were wild horses in North America thousands of years ago, but they were probably extinct long before European settlers brought horses from Eurasia in the 1500s. Some imported horses escaped to the prairies and turned wild. You can still see these mustangs in certain areas.

Life on the Move

High on the steppes of Mongolia, people live as **nomadic** herders rather than settled farmers. They spend their entire lives on the move, driving their livestock from place to place in search of fresh pasture. This way of life evolved centuries ago—the weather in this remote wilderness is too extreme and unpredictable for other types of farming. Cattle cannot survive on the steppes, so the Mongolian herders keep only sheep, goats, and yaks. Yaks are heavier and tougher than ordinary cows, with extremely thick, shaggy coats that keep out the biting wind.

The herders carry all their belongings with them, traveling on Bactrian (two-humped) camels. A few now use motorbikes to get around, but camels don't break down and are better on steep terrain. The herders camp in round tents called gers (yurts), which are

The Silk Road

The Silk Road stretched for 11,200 kilometers (7,000 miles) along the southern edge of the steppes between the Mediterranean and China. Merchants bought silk in the Xi'an region of China and then set off along the Silk Road with their camels to sell it in European markets. On the way, the trail climbed mountain passes and crossed the vast deserted steppes of central Asia. Forged during the Roman Empire, the Silk Road became the world's first great trade route.

windproof and easy to put up and carry. Gers are made of canvas stretched over a lightweight wooden frame, with a hole at the top to let out smoke from fires. For fuel, the herders burn yak dung—nothing is wasted. Inside a ger it is warm enough to sit in shirtsleeves even when it is freezing outside.

Bison Hunters

Far away on the western prairies, Native American tribes such as the Blackfoot, Crow, Cheyenne, Pawnee, and Arapaho also lived as nomads. They moved from place to place on horseback, but they were hunters rather than herders. Instead of keeping cattle, these Native Americans tracked the great migratory herds of bison.

Each group had a detailed knowledge of the landscape, and elders passed down this knowledge to the next generation. They knew exactly where the bison would be at different times of year. The trackers were always on the lookout for signs that herds had been in the area. Bison are very wary animals, so the Native Americans' only hope of catching and killing them was to launch a

Grassland Empire

Ghenghis Khan was perhaps the greatest empire builder the world has ever seen. He united various Mongol tribes and became their leader. In the first part of the 13th century, the Mongolian leader commanded a ferocious force of horseback warriors on the steppes of central Asia. Ghenghis Khan's army conquered all the peoples living between Turkey and China to create an empire that stretched from the Mediterranean to the Pacific. In addition, his descendants created the Mughal Empire of India.

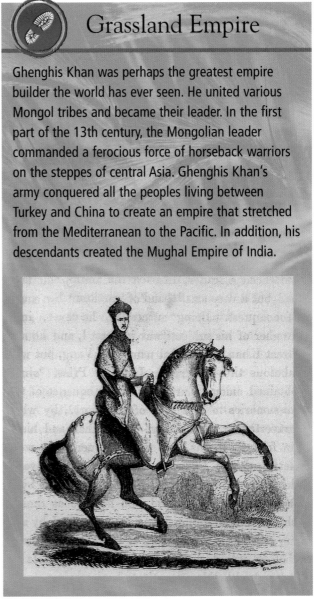

During the 19th century, settlers arrived on the American prairies by the million, and much of this vast natural grassland was tamed in less than a century.

surprise attack. A successful bison kill might take days or even weeks of patient tracking and planning.

Bison provided the Native Americans with nearly everything they needed. Besides eating the rich meat, they used the skins for clothing, blankets, and tepees; the bones to make arrows and tools such as needles; the tendons for stringing their wooden bows; and the dung for fuel.

Struggles for Land

When settlers arrived in the West, the Native Americans traded with them to get rifles and manufactured goods. However, as more newcomers set up home and their farms grew larger, they pushed the Native Americans off most of their land. The Native Americans' last armed rebellion against troops of the United States government finally collapsed in 1890.

People have fought over land in many other temperate grasslands. In the 19th century, European settlers traveled inland from the coasts of eastern Australia in search of land to farm. They reached the wild bush country known as the outback—the ancient homeland of the Aborigines. The Aborigines can trace their origins further back than any other people alive today. Some artifacts their ancestors made are at least 40,000 years old. However, determined to tame the land and create a new life for themselves, European pioneers seized the best areas of the rangeland, forcing the Aborigines to take refuge in the driest, most barren parts of the

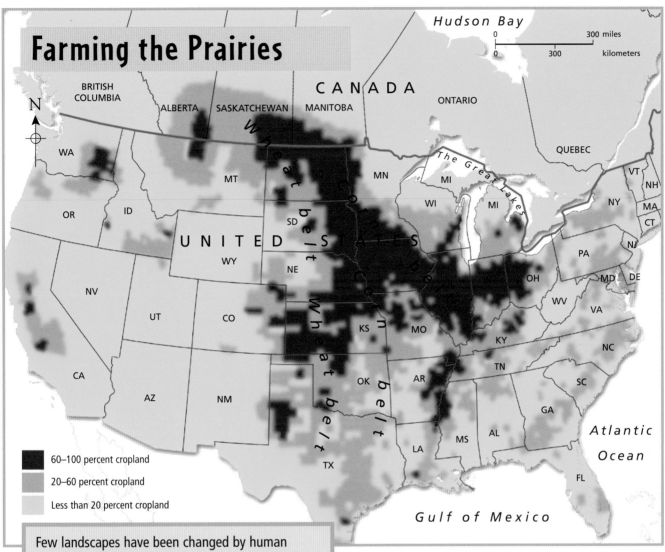

Farming the Prairies

Hudson Bay

0 — 300 miles
0 — 300 kilometers

BRITISH COLUMBIA

N

C A N A D A

ALBERTA   SASKATCHEWAN   MANITOBA

ONTARIO

QUEBEC

Wheat belt

WA

MT

U N I T E D   S T A T E S

ND

MN

MI

WI

MI

The Great Lakes

VT

NH

OR

ID

SD

Corn belt

NY

MA

CT

WY

NE

PA

NJ

NV

UT

CO

IN

OH

MD

DE

Wheat belt

KS

MO

WV

VA

CA

AZ

NM

OK

AR

KY

TN

NC

SC

TX

MS

AL

GA

Atlantic Ocean

LA

FL

■ 60–100 percent cropland

▨ 20–60 percent cropland

□ Less than 20 percent cropland

Gulf of Mexico

Few landscapes have been changed by human activity so quickly and so thoroughly as the prairies. Barely 150 years ago, natural prairie covered 40 percent of the United States. Now 99 percent is gone, and much of it has been plowed up to grow crops. Today, the prairies are North America's major cropland region, as the map above shows. What was once tallgrass prairie has become the great corn-growing region, known as the corn belt. What was once mixed-grass prairie became the wheat belt, where huge machines reap the harvest from fields of gold stretching as far as the eye can see. Once harvested, grain is stored in "prairie skyscrapers," huge silos dotted around the plains. More recently, vast areas of prairie have turned bright yellow in early summer with the blooms of canola, grown for its seeds, which are crushed to make cooking oil.

outback. Today, the Aborigines have rights as Australian citizens, but the rangeland is still essentially farmed by white Australians.

Balancing Act

The temperate grassland biome is very sensitive to changes in weather and climate. Grasses flourish where there is just enough rain for plants to survive, but not enough for forest. If the rains fail, the grasses soon disappear and the land can turn to desert.

In the past, peoples like the Native Americans, Mongolian shepherds, and Australian Aborigines lived in balance with their grassland home. Their small populations and nomadic lifestyles had less impact on the

53

Senseless Slaughter

Native Americans killed only as many bison as they needed, and their hunting had little impact on overall bison numbers. However, the hunters who moved to the Midwest from the east coast were not so careful. They shot as many bison as they could because they didn't think the immense herds could possibly run out. At that time, there was a big demand for fresh meat to feed the thousands of workers laying tracks for the new railroads. Bison made easy targets for hunters equipped with modern high-powered rifles, and they were slaughtered by the thousand. The hunters killed so many that the massive carcasses were often left lying on the plain, unclaimed.

Until the slaughter started, there were as many as 60 million bison. By 1885, the population had fallen to just 2,000. Conservationists then started to protect the remaining bison. There are about 15,000 wild bison on the prairies today and as many as 500,000 in captivity, mostly raised for their meat, which is leaner than beef.

environment than a modern agricultural way of life, and they could escape the effects of drought simply by moving on.

Today, much of the world's temperate grassland biome is a kind of artificial grassland, dominated by cereal crops that are cultivated and harvested on a vast scale. We have come to depend on this highly productive land so much that we are more susceptible than ever to its unpredictable climate.

Dust Bowl

During the 1930s, a severe drought hit the prairies, turning a huge region into a desolate wasteland: the Dust Bowl. For five years, there was little rain. Hot, dry winds made the situation worse by blowing away the loose soil. Massive clouds of choking dust rose into the sky to a height of 6,000 meters (20,000 feet), suffocating birds in midair. Many people died of heatstroke and breathing problems.

The Dust Bowl was the most tragic drought in American history. People's livelihoods turned to dust. Thousands of ruined farmers from Oklahoma packed their possessions and headed west for California. They took part in one of the biggest human migrations ever seen in North America. Some scientists believe that climate change is leading to drier conditions on the prairies, which increases the risk of a new Dust Bowl developing.

Above: The tragedy of the 1930s Dust Bowl showed what can happen when prairie soil, which takes 400 years to develop, is stripped of its protective covering of grasses.

Below: Even though wheat is a grass, wheat fields are very different from natural grassland. The rich variety of prairie plants is replaced with just a single species.

AUSTRALIAN RANGELAND

The rangeland of southeastern Australia is the warmest and driest temperate grassland of all. It merges into sandy desert on both its northern and western frontiers.

Rangeland Facts

▲ Australia's rangeland includes parts of two states—New South Wales and Victoria. It is one of the main farming regions in the world.

▲ There are patches of eucalyptus trees all over the rangeland. They grow even in very dry conditions.

▲ The Australian plague locust is a grasshopper-like insect that breeds in immense numbers every few years. During outbreaks, gigantic swarms of locusts sweep through the rangeland, eating every plant.

A World Apart

Australia was once joined to the other continents, but over millions of years it separated and drifted away. Cut off from the rest of the world, its animals and plants evolved into hundreds of unusual species, found nowhere else. Among them are the strange grass trees, also named blackboys for their dark trunks. In spring, their spearlike flower stalks, covered with masses of white flowers, shoot to a height of up to 3 meters (10 feet). The rangeland's unique animals include the gray kangaroo and the emu—a flightless bird that stands as tall as a man.

The Australian rangeland has proved an incredibly rich resource for farming sheep. There are now 140 million sheep in Australia, mainly in the rangeland.

1. Flinders Ranges
The barren hills of the Flinders Ranges are the final barrier between the rangeland and the enormous, scorching deserts that lie in the center of the continent. A proposed uranium mine in the Arkaroola Wilderness Sanctuary, within the ranges, threatens wildlife.

2. Broken Hill
There are big zinc and lead mines outside this small town, located near the desert frontier.

3. Murray River
Australia's longest and most important river flows 2,589 kilometers (1,609 miles) from the Australian Alps to the ocean near Adelaide. Unlike many of the rangeland's smaller rivers, the Murray River never dries up. Fertilizers washing into the river affect aquatic life.

4. Inland Plains
In the western half of New South Wales, the land is much too hot and dry for crops but makes good grazing. There are many, many times more sheep than people in this area. Introduced foxes prey on native animals.

5. Murray–Darling Basin
Scattered throughout the rangeland are many wetland areas, fed by water from the Murray–Darling river system.

6. Darling, Lachlan, and Murrumbidgee Rivers
These major rivers flow westward, eventually joining the Murray River.

7. Darling Downs
Fields of wheat, oats, and sugarcane cover the fertile land on either side of the Darling River's upper reaches, west of Brisbane. The Darling Downs hopping mouse is now thought to be extinct. The earless dragon—a lizard—is also at risk of extinction in the downs.

8. Great Dividing Range
In the east, a long range of forested mountains rises out of the lowlands. It divides the inland plains from the Pacific Ocean.

9. Western Foothills
The western slopes of the Great Dividing Range are a region of gentle, rolling hills. The pink-tailed worm-lizard is under threat of extinction from introduced predators such as cats and dogs.

10. Wagga Wagga
Wagga Wagga is the center of the rangeland's livestock industry, handling more than 1.5 million sheep a year.

11. Australian Alps
The highest mountains in the Great Dividing Range are known as the Australian Alps. In the Snowy Mountains here, snow covers the upper slopes in winter (June to September).

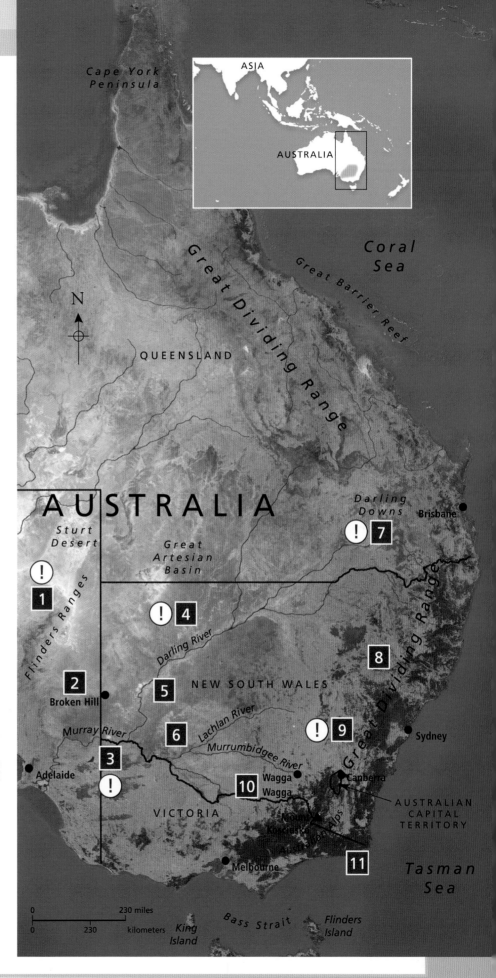

THE FUTURE

People have changed much of the world's temperate grassland to farmland, but moves are afoot to restore some areas of wild grassland to their former glory.

Billions of people across the world depend on the temperate grassland biome for their daily bread. But as the population of the world increases, there are more and more mouths to feed. Producing enough food to go around puts tremendous pressure on the plants, wildlife, and people of temperate grasslands.

Going, Going, Gone

Temperate grasslands used to cover more than a quarter of Earth's land, but over millions of years they shrank due to changes in the planet's climate. Despite this, temperate grasslands still make up one of the biggest land biomes.

However, the grassland biome has changed. Huge areas that were once grassland are now fields of crops or pasture. The flat land is great for building factories, towns, and cities, and for transportation links such as railroads and highways. Now only small patches of totally wild habitat are left. The natural prairies and pampas are down to just 1–2 percent of their original size, and 70 percent of Africa's veld is now farmland.

A grassland may look entirely natural to us, but the chances are that humans have transformed it. Heavily grazed grasslands often appear lush and healthy. However, their turf is much less varied.

Grazing by cattle, sheep, and goats keeps the vegetation extra short. It also kills off many plants—mainly nongrass species including those that bear colorful flowers. The grazed turf supports fewer insects and

other animals. But with just the right number of cattle, sheep, or goats in each area, wildlife and livestock can often exist side by side.

Sometimes ranchers deliberately sow their pasture with different grass seeds, changing the turf altogether. They select varieties that provide the best grazing for their animals. Introduced grasses dominate the pampas, for example. The original grasses, herbs, and flowers cover only a tiny fraction of the pampas. Nevertheless, although the pampas we see today is an artificial habitat, it is still a type of temperate grassland.

Creating New Habitats

Though wild areas of grassland have changed or disappeared, people are creating new grasslands all the time. Whenever we cut down woodland, clear bushes and scrub, or drain marshes, it's not long before the first wild grasses start to appear. Soon more types of plants arrive on the scene, and the cleared area gradually turns into a grassland. If the

In Vermont, as elsewhere, forest clearance has created new artificial grasslands, but the survival of native species like the northern leopard frog is threatened.

land is left alone, the turf gets wilder and richer with every passing year. Eventually, it will revert to scrub and then woodland, if new shoots are not continually cropped by grazing animals or lawnmowers.

People have been making new grasslands for thousands of years. Early humans began to cut down forests because they needed timber for firewood and building, and grass for their cattle. The continual grazing, mowing, and clearing stopped trees from returning and kept the land open. In other words, people have been turning other biomes into temperate grassland for a very long time. The green meadows of New England were once all woodland, for instance. But these new grasslands are entirely artificial.

Winners and Losers

Human activity has a dramatic impact on grassland plants and animals. Some species cannot cope with the changes to their habitat and become less common. They may even vanish from wide areas or become extinct. However, other plants and animals benefit from the changes. Sometimes, they do so well that they become a real nuisance.

 Gone with the Wind

Gales and torrential downpours can spell disaster for farmers by blowing and washing away the valuable top layer of soil. The topsoil sometimes piles up in strange places. In Kansas, a state highway department once had to remove almost 1,000 metric tons (1,100 tons) of dirt from a stretch of road just 460 meters (500 yards) long.

One way of saving the soil is to plant lines of trees as windbreaks (right.) Eucalyptus trees from Australia and fir trees are used because they grow fast and cope well with the dry climate. But native trees are a better choice because they are adapted to local conditions and provide food for wildlife.

The worst nuisance species are often those that people have introduced to a new area, far from their native range. In their new home, introduced species may have few natural enemies, such as diseases or predators, allowing them to multiply rapidly out of control.

One example is the European rabbit, which people took to Australia in the 1800s and released for hunting. Rabbits can live in all kinds of places, but meadows and fields of grass are just perfect. When conditions are right, they breed with amazing speed.

The warm grasslands of Australia suited rabbits so well that there are now nearly a billion of them there. Major farmland pests, they not only destroy crops and pasture but also upset the local ecosystem and drive out other species. Among the casualties are the greater bilby, which is now an endangered species, and the burrowing bettong, which is now entirely extinct on the mainland.

Looking to the Future

Some of the surviving patches of natural temperate grassland in North America are now protected as reserves or national parks. A few are huge. Grasslands National Park preserves 910 square kilometers (350 square miles) of original prairie in Saskatchewan, Canada, for instance. New prairie reserves are popping up all over North America, and

Farming of the Future

All over the world, people are trying out new ways of using grasslands. In Australia and North America, a growing number of farms keep flocks of emus and ostriches (left). The birds provide low-fat meat and giant eggs weighing 0.9 kilograms (2 pounds) each, as well as masses of fluffy feathers. There are even plans to turn emu oil into a moisturizing cream. Emus and ostriches are ideal for farming because they don't need much looking after. In the African veld, there are experiments to keep herds of native antelope. Antelope can survive tougher conditions than either cattle or sheep and do less damage to wild plants.

tiny pockets of prairie still survive in some surprising places, such as in cemeteries and beside railroad tracks and highways.

Many biologists hope to reintroduce some of the animals that once dominated North America's temperate grasslands. Tule elks and pronghorns have been reintroduced to California's central valley grasslands, and bison are making a comeback in Yellowstone National Park, where gray wolves have also been reintroduced. There is even a proposal for a 360,000-square-kilometer (130,000-square-mile) "Buffalo Commons," allowing bison to roam freely over the prairies of several states, including Oklahoma and Kansas.

Wild grasslands are worth saving for people as well as for animals. People visit them to enjoy the scenery; go hiking, hunting, and horseback riding; and to watch the wildlife. Temperate grasslands can still be a marvelous resource for leisure, farming, and industry, but only if we plan ahead and treat them wisely.

People's love of grasslands for hiking and other leisure activities will help preserve this biome for future generations to enjoy.

Saving the Planet

As more and more temperate grasslands are taken over by farms, many of their rich array of plants are becoming very rare and even flowering meadow species (below) are becoming increasingly endangered by changes in farming practice. In Europe, for instance, many once-common meadow species such as cornflowers are now hard to find. However, if the seeds of these plants are stored properly, they can sprout into perfect plants decades later. This gave scientists the idea for the Millennium Seed Bank in Kew Gardens in England. The Seed Bank is a project to collect, catalog, and store the seeds of 10 percent of the world's flowering plants—which it achieved in 2009. That's a total of more than 24,000 species. In the future some of these plants might turn out to produce life-saving medicines. Another use for the seeds could be to breed new strains of fruits and crops.

GLOSSARY

adaptation: Characteristic feature of an animal or plant developed through evolution in keeping with changes in circumstances.

biome: A major division of the living world, distinguished by its climate and wildlife. Tundra, desert, and temperate grasslands are examples of biomes.

blizzard: A severe snowstorm with very high winds (above 51 km/h 32 km/h) and temperatures below 20°F (-6.7°C) that cuts visibility to less than 152 meters (500 feet).

bulb: A kind of fattened root used by a plant for storage of food.

bush: Wild, unsettled areas of Australia and Africa.

carbon dioxide: A gas released when fuel burns. It is one of the main gases causing global warming.

carnivore: Animal that survives primarily by eating other animals.

chlorophyll: A green chemical in the leaves and stems of plants that captures the energy in sunlight and helps convert it to food.

climate: The pattern of weather that happens in one place during an average year.

cold-blooded: Having a body temperature that depends on the surroundings. Reptiles are cold-blooded, for example. *See also* warm-blooded.

convergent evolution: Process by which completely different species develop similar traits in response to similar conditions.

desert: A biome that receives less than 250 millimeters (10 inches) of rain a year.

domestic animal: An animal kept by people, usually as a pet, farm animal, or pack animal.

dormant: So inactive as to appear lifeless. Many animals become dormant to survive times of stress, such as cold spells and droughts.

equator: An imaginary line around Earth, midway between the poles.

estivation: A time of dormancy some animals such as amphibians go through in summer to help them survive drought and heat.

evaporate: To turn into gas. When water evaporates, it becomes an invisible part of the air.

fertile: Soil that is capable of sustaining plant growth is termed fertile. Farmers try to make soil more fertile when growing crops.

global warming: The gradual warming of Earth's climate, caused by pollution of the atmosphere.

hemisphere: One half of Earth. The northern hemisphere is the half to the north of the equator.

herbaceous plant: A plant that has no woody tissue. Many herbaceous plants die back in winter.

hibernation: A time of dormancy that some animals go through during winter. In true hibernation, the heart rate and breathing slow dramatically and the body cools.

humus: Vital, dark brown organic matter in the soil created by animal dung and the rotting remains of plants and animals.

ice age: A period when Earth's climate was cooler and the polar ice caps expanded. The last ice age ended 10,000 years ago.

metabolism: An animal's or plant's chemical process of breaking down food to release energy.

microclimate: The pattern of weather within a small area, such as a valley, treetop, or burrow.

migration: A long-distance journey by an animal to find a new home. Many animals migrate each year.

nomad: A person who travels from place to place in search of food and water, instead of settling permanently.

nutrient: Any chemical in the soil that plants need.

pampas The treeless, grassy plains of temperate South America.

pollination: The transfer of pollen from the male part of a flower to the female part of the same flower or another flower, causing the flower to produce seeds.

prairie: A large area of grassland in central North America.

predator: An animal that catches and eats other animals.

protein: One of the major food groups. It is used for building and repairing plant and animal bodies.

rangeland: Open grassland in the Australian interior.

sap: The body liquid of plants.

short-grass prairie: Dry area of prairie where grasses such as buffalo grass and blue grama grow up to 50 centimeters (18 inches).

species: A particular type of organism. Cheetahs are a species, for instance, but birds are not, because there are lots of different bird species.

steppe: Vast, grassy plain in Asia and eastern Europe, often very dry.

Stone Age: A period in human prehistory when people used stone tools.

subtropical: A region of Earth within the temperate zone, but near, and similar to, the tropics. Florida is often called subtropical.

taiga: A biome in northern regions that mainly contains conifer trees.

tallgrass prairie: A moist area of prairie where grasses such as Indian grass and big blue stem grow up to 3 meters (10 feet) tall.

temperate: Between the warm tropics and the cold, polar regions.

temperate forest: A biome of the temperate zone that mainly contains broad-leaved trees.

temperate grassland: A biome of the temperate zone that mainly contains grassland.

tornado: Very violent funnel-shaped wind that sweeps across the land beneath a thundercloud.

tropic of Cancer: An imaginary line around Earth about 2,600 kilometers (1,600 miles) north of the equator.

tropic of Capricorn: An imaginary line around Earth 2,600 kilometers (1,600 miles) south of the equator.

tropical: Between the tropics of Cancer and Capricorn. Tropical countries are warm all year round.

tropical forest: Forest in Earth's tropical zone, such as tropical rain forest or monsoon forest.

tropical grassland: A tropical biome in which grass is the main form of plant life.

tundra: A biome of the far north, made up of treeless plains covered with small plants.

vapor: A gas formed when a liquid evaporates.

veld or veldt: A broad, high area of grassland in southern Africa. The word comes from the Dutch word for "field."

warm-blooded: Having a warm body temperature constantly. Mammals are warm-blooded.

Further Research

Books
Farndon, John. *The Wildlife Atlas*. New York: Reader's Digest, 2002.
Freedman, Jeri. *Grasslands (Biomes of the World)*. New York: Rosen Central, 2009.
Stille, Darlene. *Grasslands (True Books: Ecosystems)*. New York: Children's Press, 2000.
Toupin, Laurie. *Life in The Temperate Grasslands*. New York: Franklin Watts, 2005.
Wallace, Marianne D. *America's Prairies and Grasslands*. Golden, CO: Fulcrum, 2001.

Websites
Temperate Grasslands: www.radford.edu/~swoodwar/CLASSES/GEOG235/biomes/tempgrass/tempgras.html
(A concise collection of facts about temperate grasslands.)
Grasslands: www.blueplanetbiomes.org/grasslands.htm
(A useful site with information about specific grasslands.)

INDEX

Picture Credits

Key: l – left, r – right, m – middle, t – top, b – bottom.

Front cover: Shutterstock: Roger Dale Calger. **Ardea:** Bilat Yves 6r, 18/19; Mary Clay 33; John Daniels 34/35; Bob Gibbons 24b; Francois Gohier 35t, 41; Colin Monteath 47; Jim Zipp 43; **Art Explosion:** 30b, 59b; **Bruce Coleman:** Bruce Coleman Inc. 12/13, 28/29, 30/31, 36, 45; Sven Halling 7l, 58/59; HPH Photography 7ml, 32/33; Wayne Lankinen 8; Werner Layer 38; Joe McDonald 37t; Natural Selections Inc. 1, 20/21; Marie Read 40; **Corbis:** 55t; Tom Bean 6m, 22b; Gianni Dagli Orti 52; Ecoscene/Wayne Lawler 7r, 56b; Bob Krist 61; David Muench 15, 22/23; Keren Su 50/51; **Digital Stock:** World Panoramas 54/55; **Image Bank:** Eric Meola 14; Miao China Tourism Press, Wang 7mr, 46; **istockphoto:** 13t, 54t; **Jupiter:** Stockxpert 60; **Mary Evans Picture Library:** 51b; **Natural History Museum:** 18; **NHPA:** A.N.T. 26/27; Stephen Krasemann 58t; Julie Meech 56t; David Middleton 24t; Rod Planck 37b, 38/39; John Shaw 9, 48/49; **PhotoDisc:** Alan and Sandy Carey 44; Robert Glusic 4m; Bruce Heinemann 5l; Jack Hollingsworth 5m; Photolink 5r, 27 (inset); Karl Weatherley 4r; Public Domain: 32 (inset); **Shutterstock:** Chrisa DeRidder 25b; Veranis 39m; **Still Pictures:** Keith Kent 10/11; Stephen Pern 49b; Roland Seitre 42; **Stone:** Terry Donnelly 29t; Charles Doswell III 16.

The Brown Reference Group Ltd. has made every attempt to contact the copyright holder. If anyone has any information please contact info@brownreference.com